THE GREAT COMMISSION

Joseph K. Jok

 A catalogue record for this book is available from the National Library of Australia

Copyright © 2019 Joseph K. Jok

All rights reserved worldwide.

No part of the book may be copied or changed in any format, sold, or used in a way other than what is outlined in this book, under any circumstances, without the prior written permission of the publisher.

This edition published by Africa World Books
www.africaworldbooks.com.au

Nation Library of Australia Cataloguing-in-Publication entry

Author: Jok, Joseph K.

Title: THE GREAT COMMISSION/ Joseph K. Jok

ISBN: 978-0-6485028-3-8

Contents

Acknowledgements 4

Introduction 5

Chapter 1: God's original plan 7

Chapter 2: Adam's origin 13

Chapter 3: Beyond the naked eyes 22

Chapter 4: God's image and likeness 33

Chapter 5: What is a Kingdom? 37

Chapter 6: The Great commission 57

Chapter 7: The power of the gospel 66

Chapter 8: Salvation the seal of dominion 81

Acknowledgements

I want to give special thanks to my family, friends and everyone who has helped me make this project a success. Without the support of these people around me it wouldn't be possible for me to accomplish the mission God has laid on my heart, to write this book which I believe will transform many lives. Lastly and most importantly, I give honour and glory to my Lord Jesus Christ who has enabled me and given me this opportunity to be vessel in his hands; without Him I wouldn't have been who I am today. I give Him glory for the strength, courage, wisdom and boldness He gave me to write this book, to God be the glory.

This work is a result of learning from the word of God, development from mentors, supporters, pastors, friends and family who have invested their time, resources, energy and interest in my dreams and calling. I am forever grateful.

No achievements, success, or progress in life is without the support and the help of people. We have all been impacted one way or another through someone whom God brought into our life. Once again, I thank God for everyone who have been part of this journey who supported this project to completion, I believe it will bless, change and transform the lives of many people globally. Glory be to God.

Introduction

Salvation is not an escape route to heaven but a seal of dominion on earth over the devil, sin, sickness, disease, poverty and death. The original intention of God creating humans was never for humankind to live in heaven but on earth as a duplicate of Him. This book will reveal key aspects about God's original plan, redemption and how to release the supernatural kingdom of God on earth through the authority and power given to sons and daughters in the kingdom. Nowadays many people including Christians have misconceptions about God's original plan because of the lack of kingdom revelation. The bible is a story about a loving king and his kingdom being expanded through His image and likeness in humankind. Therefore, throughout reading this book, you will discover and learn truths about your identity, purpose, assignment, inheritance and dominion. Our present life here on earth should reflect kingdom culture and its power. As the body of Christ, God in His divine and infinite wisdom has given us the responsibility and assignment to make Him known and establish His kingdom on earth as it is in heaven. The mystery of God entrusting us to represent Him was hidden in Christ Jesus before time began. But is now revealed to His sons and daughters whom He wants equipped and established to bring infiltration and change to every aspect of society through the power of

His Spirit. This mystery hidden in Christ was that the manifold wisdom of God be made known to principalities and powers in the heavenly places through the church; this wisdom is Jesus in whom God restored all things unto Himself. The book (Isaiah 60:1-4) gives us a prophetic insight concerning our role as the triumphant church of Jesus Christ, returning to the original mandate God gave to Adam. To possess the earth, the nations, and bring a transformation in the whole world in this last hour as ambassadors of Christ before the second coming of the Lord Jesus.

(All bible references will be from the NKJV and NLT unless otherwise stated).

Chapter 1
God's original plan

In our society, today the majority of people struggle in life simply because they have not yet realised the abilities, resources and potential God has hidden within their spirit person. Humans, by nature are not the strongest beings physically on the earth realm; we have gigantic animals such as elephants, bears, lions, tigers and so forth which can crush a person instantly, but God created humankind to be the most powerful beings in the entire universe, that the whole creation listens and obeys the sound of His voice (Genesis 1:26-28). We see Adam exercising this level of authority and dominion in Genesis 2:18-20; he named all the animals without even having any prior knowledge about animals. Today we have many graduates who have studied zoology and biology and still cannot have the same accurate detailed knowledge and understanding Adam had towards all the animals he named. His knowledge was divine and very accurate, in that he was very intelligent and creative like God. Adam had divine knowledge in his spirit and he also had the imagination of God operating in him; his thoughts process and perceptions were connected to the mind of God whereby he had the accurate wisdom and the imagination of God in his life and he clearly demonstrated this when it came to naming all the animals. I believe Adam could see and know every time he gave each animal a name, what God would have called that animal. All the names he gave to the animals whether sea creatures, birds of the air, beasts and animals on the land, mammals and cold blooded were very accurate. In this situation, God never intervened or corrected him for making any error regarding naming all the animals, and that was his first time, which was remarkable. Another insight here evident is in the introduction of Eve. When God put Adam into a deep sleep, He took one of his ribs out and created the woman with it. Therefore, what I want to highlight here is not the nice romantic words Adam spoke to Eve which were "bone of my bones flesh of my flesh" but rather the accuracy of his knowledge, that even while he was in a deep sleep he was still accurate in articulating and defining the woman God brought to him from his ribs, without any informed knowledge passed unto him when he woke up. What is remarkable is that Adam said, (Genesis 2:23), "She shall be called woman because she was taken out of Man." And while God made the woman out of his rib while he was sleeping, this is the divine wisdom of God operating in Adam which has always been God's plan for humanity to operate in His divine knowledge (2 Peter 1:3).

In Genesis 1:28 God gave humankind four specific assignments to fulfil the mandate He gave them here on earth. The first one which I will explore and expound on is **Dominion**. The word **dominion** means**, strength, might and power;** it's where we get the word **domain** which speaks of territory, province, area or a zone where a king rules. God's original plan was to stretch His kingdom and His dominion on earth as it is in heaven through humankind. In the mind of God, earth is a colony of heaven that

God's original plan

He wanted the humankind family to enlarge His kingdom. God's eternal mission on earth was to expand His kingdom through humanity, which is a wonderful privilege. In His sovereign choice, He picked us instead of other celestial beings such as angels. He did this because He wanted His own image and likeness to expand His kingdom through establishing His plan, purpose and will. Just as it is in the natural, you will never see kingly inheritance given to common people but rather only the sons and daughters of the King and the royal family who inherits the throne and the authority. Because it is legally in their DNA to be royal, this also applies to a child of God. We are born into a royal family whereby we are kings and priests ruling and reigning with our Lord Jesus Christ. Everything God created He spoke into existence, but for humankind He carefully thought about him. What a privilege! Genesis 1:26, "Then God said, 'Let us make man in our own image; according to Our likeness let them have dominion'". This is the ideal model and intention of God for humankind to be rulers and have dominion on earth as it is in heaven. As you will notice in Genesis chapter one when God created humankind, he was the only being that possessed two qualities which other created beings did not have both celestial and terrestrial; these were image and likeness. The image and likeness of God are what sets humankind apart from creation and gives us the qualifications to have dominion and supremacy over all creation because we represent God. The authority of humankind is hidden in his identity. I believe Adam glowed with the glory of God before the fall, and whenever he moved around the garden the whole creation would witness the glory of God glowing through him as he bore the image of God bodily (Psalms 8:4-6). Although having a physical body he was not dominated by his senses but by the Spirit of God through his inner man (Proverbs 20:27). It was the presence of God that Adam carried that gave him authority over the whole creation; he was literally a *small god* as Psalms 82:6 states.

Fruitfulness: God created Adam to be fruitful like Him. We think of fruitfulness only regarding procreation, but God had a bigger picture. The Lord wanted Adam to be fruitful in everything – his health, relationships, mind, work, emotions, wealth and life. There are two aspects to a fruit; firstly the harvest and secondly the seed. Within every fruit there is a future and that is what we call a seed, and secondly the harvest which speaks of pleasure, to enjoy what has fully grown and ripened. God never intended for humankind to be barren and limited in life; lack and barrenness were both consequences of the fall. God's will for us is to prosper and be fruitful in all areas of our lives, this means wherever we go we are meant to be fruitful and successful. We carry the life of God on the inside of us, it is the abundant lifestyle full of fruitfulness and quality of living. God promised that wherever we step, the sole of our feet we shall possess (Joshua 1:3).

Multiplication and Duplication: The Garden of Eden was the starting point of Adam for expanding the invisible King and His kingdom on earth. This was an assignment and a command God gave humankind, part of the multiplication was reproducing children but not only that alone. God wanted His qualities and attributes to be passed down generations by his word and presence. Duplication is quality and pattern of the same kind reproduced. God created humanity to duplicate all His qualities, values, principles into their/our descendants to know Him as the Lord God almighty who created them in His image and likeness and gave the universe as an inheritance as His legal representatives on earth.

Rulership: humanity, was created with an inbuilt desire to rule and lead because it is in our nature that we inherited from our

God's original plan

creator. Part of this ruling is seen when the Lord set Adam to look after the Garden of Eden. The Lord God said, "Let them have dominion over the earth" which referred both to Adam and Eve. Psalms 8:6-8 says, "The Lord God has put all things under man's feet that which He has created and gave him the right to rule over all His creation on earth". This is fascinating and awesome as it shows His amazing love; He created all things for us to enjoy, and created us in His image and likeness, so that when creation sees us it beholds the image of God in us.

These four assignments reveal and paint the picture of humanity's identity, purpose and assignment. The vision of the Father in creation was to duplicate Himself in humanity. It is captivating when you think about how you are created in the image and the likeness of the creator. This itself should give a hint of how powerful and important you are to your creator. The purpose of God for creation revolves around humankind and without humanity on earth everything in creation loses value; you are the masterpiece of God's creation (see Ephesians 2:10). You were in the mind of your heavenly father before creation (see Jeremiah 1:5). This scripture unveils the omniscient ability of God in knowing all things and it shows the love He has for us and of His perfect knowledge of your potential and purpose. Hereby we can use the example of Apple and their products constantly produced in their factories. For instance whenever a new IPhone comes out in the market, it usually comes with a small manual book that carries on it instructions to help the user have basic knowledge and understanding of how to operate the new IPhone purchased. This means that Apple did not discover the purpose of IPhones after creating them but before its creation. So then the IPhone becomes the fulfilment of the purpose which is to help people communicate, have entertainment, and access to the internet.

What this example implies is that God did not create humankind to find a purpose but rather for a purpose as a duplicate of his class of function as a god on earth. Humankind is the rightful and legal ruler of the earth because God his Father has legally assigned it to him to exercise dominion and rulership as it was the original mandate God assigned to Adam.

Chapter 2
Adam's origin

The book of Genesis reveals an insight about God assigning the earth to Adam legally (1:26). God said, "Let **them** have dominion". The words **let them** here are very important to highlight because it states that God has given humankind dominion over the earth which is His original plan. Genesis 1:26-28 reflects God as creator; He modelled the lifestyle of dominion and authority in creation to show and teach humanity what it really means to be made in His image and likeness. (Genesis 1:26-28 NLT 26) "Then God said, 'Let us make human beings in our image, to be like us. They will reign over the fish in the sea, the birds in the sky, the livestock, all the wild animals on earth, and the small animals that scurry along the ground.'" All the animals that God created were after their own kind that is why a lion behaves like a lion instinctively because it is built naturally in its DNA. The same applies to human beings as it is in procreation where a father's DNA and genetics can be passed down to a son or daughter, which is remarkable and interesting truth because this principle of duplication is found in everything God created on earth. You will never find a lion one day behaving like a dog unless something is wrong in the genetic code; animals such as birds, mammals and fish produce after their own kind naturally. This gives us a clear understanding that humankind carries the DNA of God within with instincts to be like God, because it is built in us naturally. Another analogy would be that of a child. Every child born has no control and choice over their features and appearance when they are born, even though most times they end up looking like their parents, so the point is that they still carry the DNA of their father. So, humankind carries the nature of God and DNA naturally. We were created by our heavenly Father for a divine purpose and an eternal relationship with Him as He duplicated His qualities in us because He loves us beyond imagination and anything we could ever experience. Apostle Paul expresses this divine relationship in his writing to the church of Rome by saying "What can separate us from the love of God in Christ, neither death nor life, nor angels nor principalities nor powers, nor things present nor things to come, nor height nor depth, nor any other created thing, shall be able to separate us from the love of God in Christ Jesus" (Romans 8:37-39) (Ephesians 3:18-19). In the gospel of John, we see the divinity of our Lord Jesus Christ (John 1:1-3). Jesus is the word of God who became flesh. John reveals it with insight whereby he writes (John 1:1), "In the beginning was the Word and the Word was with God and the Word was God". It shows that Jesus is the **complete revelation and manifestation** of the Father. Through Him we understand and see the nature of God the Father, who He is and His heart towards humanity (see Colossians 1:15) (see John 3:16). In every area of Jesus Christ's life you see the Father and His intention vividly. There are two main biblical descriptions of God in the bible, firstly God is love and secondly God is light. These two great descriptions are clearly seen in Jesus Christ.

Through his work of atonement He has reconciled and restored us into the kingdom family through His blood on the cross of Calvary. The life of Jesus is the visible pattern of the original plan God had for humanity as He is our only true example and saviour whereby He lived a complete supernatural life. He dominated and defeated Satan once and for all, He modelled to us how dominion and authority should be exercised as children of God. Jesus Christ conquered Satan, sin, death and the grave and restored everything Adam lost with authority. He was Christ the healer, the great physician who healed all who came to Him, Christ the saviour, saving the lost, and Christ the deliverer and redeemer. Thus through His redemptive work He redeemed us from all the works of the evil one Satan. Every child of God has the access and legal rights to possess everything Satan has stolen from them through the authority given to them in the name of Jesus our High Priest. Jesus conquered Satan as man not as God; even though He was God He dropped all his divine privileges, He lived dependently on the Holy Spirit and He submitted His will to the Father. As the Son, He became human and humbled Himself and became obedient to the Father even to the point of death, therefore He was highly exalted as the King of Kings and Lord of Lords (see Philippians 2:8). The bible makes it clear that the moment Jesus was baptised by John the Baptist, the Holy Spirit came and rested on Him from that moment onwards His ministry started. This goes to show us that Jesus set an example before us that we should follow in all areas of our lives. Every believer has living within, the same Spirit that raised Christ Jesus from the dead (Acts 10:38). The Spirit of God anoints us just like Jesus was anointed by the Father, to walk in the power of the Holy Spirit and live the life of dominion and as He is, so are we on this earth.

Understanding humankind identity

Understanding the true identity of humankind has been the most complicated quest for many. The answer to the question, Who am I? remains a mystery until God steps in; it takes the revelation of the Holy Spirit to understand who humanity is. False identity is the reason many live oppressed, depressed, defeated and bound. The word of God reveals to us the identity of humans as spirit beings with a soul and who live in a body (see 1 Thessalonians 5:23). Over the years humankind has used theories, such as evolution theory, big bang theory, science, family lineage and ancestral beliefs to trace down the origin of their roots. These man-made theories have increased and caused more confusion on the identity of humankind. When people do not understand their identity based on God's word, Satan can rob them from their destiny, dreams, visions and inheritance through ignorance and lies they believed about themselves. In the book of Acts chapter 19 we read about the story of the seven sons of Sceva in Ephesus. They saw Paul being used mightily by the Lord in a great revival, whereby the people of that region were being delivered into the kingdom of God through the ministry of the Apostle Paul. These brothers imitated the Apostle Paul without the understanding of his calling as an anointed servant of God called to the ministry. They observed Paul using the name of Jesus to cast out evil spirits and they assumed that was the formula to possess supernatural power to be like Paul. At that moment they attempted to imitate Paul in casting out evil spirits in the name of Jesus and the evil spirits answered to them saying, "Jesus I know and Paul I know, but who are you?". The scriptures go onto say that they were over-powered by the man whom the evil spirit possessed and were shamed (see Acts 19:13-16). This example shows the importance of knowing your identity in Jesus Christ. Satan does not care if you know all the bible scriptures or attend church regularly, he only submits under the feet of those who know and exercise their rights and authority as sons and daughters of the most-high God. The sons of Sceva thought spiritual things were a joke. Paul knew who he was and demonstrated this throughout all his ministry as a spiritual giant in the faith. The gospel of Saint John 8:31-33 NKJV, "Then Jesus said to those Jews who believed Him, 'if you abide in My word, you are my disciples indeed'". 32 "And you shall know the truth, and the truth shall make you free". 33 "They answered Him, 'We are Abraham's descendants and have never been in bondage to anyone. How can you say, 'You will be made free'?". In this passage the scripture unveils a wonderful truth about how true freedom comes through the knowledge of the word of God inspired by the Holy Spirit, and in alignment to the subject, many have not yet discovered who they really are in regards to their new creation identity in Christ Jesus (see 1 Corinthians 5:17). When you lack the knowledge of your true self it creates a life full of many bondages, which can be spiritual, mental, emotional, financial, relational and physical. The true knowledge of your identity reveals your **purpose**, **potential**, **assignment** and **position**. Many people are not living within the range of their purpose and potential not because the devil is hindering them **but** rather because they do not understand who they are in Christ. The bible gives us insight about who humankind is. Genesis 1:26-27 reveals the creation of the spirit, which is the inward person no one can see with their physical eyes (1 Samuel 16:7). This is the part that returns to God when our physical bodies die. The human spirit carries God's image and likeness because God is spirit and this mean the real identity of humankind is spirit. In chapter 2:7 God creates the house or body which this spirit being called "human" lives, and the body carries the five senses sight, smell, hearing, touch and taste, and is the vehicle of the human spirit. Through the body humankind can function on earth and fulfil God's mission which is to expand His kingdom on earth. In Genesis 1: 26NKJV, "Then God said, 'Let us make man in our own image, according to our **likeness**; let **them** have dominion over the fish of the sea, over the birds of the air, and over the cattle, over all the earth and over every creeping thing that creeps on earth'. 27 So God created man in his own image; in the image of God He created them; male and female He created them." As established earlier on, everything God created was created after its own kind.

Genesis 1:11, "Then God said, 'Let the earth bring forth grass, the herb that yields seed, and the fruit tree that yields fruit according to its kind, whose seed is in itself, on earth'; and it was so. 12 And the earth brought forth grass, the herb that yields seed according to its kind, and the tree that yields fruits, whose seed is in itself according to its kind. And God saw it was good."

We can learn a principle of creation here in these verses, I describe it as the **principle of duplication,** everything God created only duplicated after their own kind; trees, herbs, grass and animals. In the same manner humankind is created after the pattern of God, or one would say in the God *class* to function as a god on earth. This is something fascinating; we see that it is only into humans that God breathed the breath of life. The God kind of life contains all the features and the attributes of God and no other being in creation carries the breath of life (see Genesis 2:7). This is so powerful because we cannot be compared with animals as some have already done through evolution theory. Humankind is not an animal or otherwise God would be too. What makes a person unique, from all the other created beings

Adam's origin

is his or her spirit which is created in the image and the likeness of God.

Humans - spirit beings

The identity of humankind is found in God. Notice God said in Genesis 1:26, "Let us make man in our own image after our own kind" which means the human identity is a spirit just as God is Spirit. The image of God in him speaks of having the same ability that God has. This is not to compare humans with the most-high God, but rather he is a small god after His likeness. Religious people consider it a heresy to say man is a god, but the bible says it in Psalms 82:6NKJV: "I said, 'You are gods, and all of you are the children of the most-high God.'" This psalm here shades truth concerning humankind identity as a **spirit being**, having a **soul** and lives in a **body**. Proverbs 20:27nkjv says, "The spirit of a man is the lamp of the LORD, searching all the inner depths of his heart". The Father relates to us through our human spirit and the attributes of the spirit are faith, hope, love and prayer. Humans are spirit beings who have **souls,** which consists of the mind, will, emotions and personality, and lastly, they live in **bodies.** The body is the house where the spirit lives and this body operates through the five senses, sight, smell, hearing, touch and taste.

2 Corinthians 4:16nkjv, "Therefore we do not lose heart. Even though our outward man is perishing, yet the inward man is being renewed daily". This scripture is talking both about the inward person and the outward person. The inward person is the real you which is your spirit and the outward person is your body – the house your spirit lives in. That is why when someone dies the body is left in the grave and the spirit returns to the spirit world which our naked eyes cannot see. 2 Corinthians 5:1-10NKJV, "For we know that if our earthly house is destroyed, we have a building

from God, a house not made with hands, eternal in the heavens". When God created humankind He designed him to be an eternal being who is immortal just like Him. The spirit of a person has the knowledge and wisdom of God, because faith is a faculty of the human spirit, and we cannot produce faith with our mind but only with our spirit.

Proverbs 23:7KJV, "For as he thinketh in his heart so is he: 'Eats and drink', saith he, but his heart is not with thee". Proverbs 27:19NKJV "As in water face reflects face, so a man's heart **reveals** the man".

We can say that the words 'heart' and 'spirit' are interchangeable because they both imply the same idea of the inner person. We know that the word 'heart' is a metaphor used many times in the word of God to express the central importance of something or the centre of something. Romans 10:9 says, "With the heart man believes", and here we know automatically through common sense that Paul is not stating that we believe with our human organ called the heart, but rather he is saying we believe with our spirit, or otherwise the born-again experience will be physical, rather than a spiritual birth (John 3:5-8). Nicodemus could not comprehend the new birth concept so he asked Jesus how can someone enter his mother's womb a second time and be born a second time? His question here states that the human mind cannot handle and comprehend the ways of God. Jesus then goes on to explain to him that the born again experience is supernatural – it is not by human logic and strength but by the power of God. It is with our spirit we commune with God, not our mind or body. Throughout history we have had different periods and dispensations where humankind went through many changes. Firstly, we had the age of physical giants where only the strong physically would dominate and it was all about physical strength.

This was the age where civilisation had not begun. Secondly, we had the age of mental giants or the age of philosophers, the age of reason where people began to use more of their minds than their physical abilities and this age lasted long until today. So, for a long-time humankind has only been exercising his body and mind. The true identity of humans revealed in God's word is spirit being, with a soul and it lives in a body. In these last days God is raising spiritual giants who will walk in the fullness of the power of the Holy Spirit dominating both in the realm of the spirit and the natural realm.

Chapter 3
Beyond the naked eyes

At one point in my journey walking with the Lord I had so many questions which were mysteries to me because at that time I did not know much about what Christ did for me through His finished work. I remember going to one of the church revival meetings which was conducted for three days and in those three days I was very hungry for the touch of God upon my life as I wanted to experience what it feels like to be caught up in the spiritual realm. I decided to attend the three days revival meeting, and the first day went and I did not experience anything, so I went home that day and prayed hard because I thought at that time it was the solution. The second day I was very excited because I believed something great was going to happen to me. I was full of expectations during the service and was very attentive and made sure I did not miss out on anything the preacher was saying. After he preached he began to flow in words of knowledge calling conditions of people with sickness and problems on that day for deliverance, healing and miracles. I saw people being healed, delivered and transformed at that moment as the congregation were standing worshipping the Lord. The Holy Spirit was moving mightily in the place as I recall myself concentrating my attention on the Lord. During the altar call given for people to be filled with the Holy Spirit I went up to the front to experience what it felt like to have a supernatural experience with Lord, and as I stood there at the altar hungry for an encounter with the Lord, I suddenly fell under the power of God, and I was unconscious for a few minutes in a trance. In that moment, I had an experience which I cannot forget in my life as I saw the Lord seated on the throne while angels were beside Him and the brightness of the place was indescribable and words cannot express the beauty and splendour that I saw in this trance experience. The light we receive from the sun, moon and electricity is not close enough to be compared with it. During that encounter, I remember zooming in to focus on the face of the Lord but the intensity of the light would not allow me to see His face. My body was down in the church and my spirit was in another realm; that moment I was in two worlds at the same time. This was the first time I had a supernatural outside body experience which left me puzzled, yet I knew it was the Lord showing me His glory to strengthen my faith in Him. On that day, I understood that this physical body we walk around with is nothing but just a house and the real person is the spirit, the hidden person that physical eyes cannot see.

2 Kings 6:15NKJV, "And when the servant of the man of God arose early and went out, there was an army, surrounding the city with horses and chariots. And his servant said, 'Alas, my Master! What shall we do?' 16 So he answered, 'Do not fear, for those who are with us are more than those who are with them.' 17 And Elisha prayed, and said 'LORD, I pray, open his eyes that he may see.' Then the LORD opened the eyes of the young man, and he saw. And behold, the mountain was full of horses and chariots of fire all around Elisha."

1 Samuel 16:6-7NKJV, "So it was, when they came, that he looked at Eliab and said, 'surely the Lord's anointed is before him!' but the Lord said to Samuel, 'don't look at his appearance or at his physical stature, because I refused him; for the Lord does not see as man sees; for man looks at the outward appearance, but the Lord looks at the heart'."

The realm of the spirit is a real realm just as real as this earth realm we live in is. The scriptures make it clear that the things which are seen, touched and felt were not made by visible means but were created by the invisible God, (Hebrews 11:3-6). The spiritual realm is more real than the physical realm; it is the realm of faith, miracles and the supernatural. Many people have been taught in science, psychology, philosophy and other forms of literature that the spiritual realm does not exist including spiritual beings such as angels and demons, spiritual places such as heaven and hell, and many have even concluded that God and Satan do not exist, with an argument that all of these are made up in the mind. This is implying a lie that we are only a mind and a body, and that we do not have a spirit, which equally puts humankind on the same level with animals. All these are human-made theories yet the word of God is the truth (1 Thessalonians 5:23). Man is a spirit being that possesses a soul, which consists of the mind, will and emotions and he lives in a body with five senses. When this very central truth of humankind's identity is denied in society, human knowledge and theories become the substitute to a big void and empty space within the hearts of people that cannot be satisfied by philosophy, science, human logic and experience. Humankind's main issues are primarily spiritual, but he has been using natural means to solve spiritual problems for thousands of years since the fall of Adam. The politicians, scientists and doctors cannot fix it, and in saying this I do not mean everything has to be spiritualised, for example when you are hungry you do not eat a spiritual meal, but instead a nice decent meal that will satisfy you from hunger. The main point here is that the root cause of humanity's problem is spiritual. In the western world people are so intellectually oriented trying to find solutions for everything within range of their human knowledge including spiritual problems. Knowledge itself is not the problem but when human knowledge is exalted above the knowledge of God, that is when it produces all kinds of problems (1 Cor. 1:18-31). No human, including the sharpest mind the world has ever seen could solve the root problem of humankind, but praise be to God that through Jesus Christ sin, death, fear and all kinds of spiritual bondages have been destroyed through His blood and resurrection. John 1:12 says, "To all those who believe in Him (Jesus Christ) He gave them the rights/authority to be called sons and daughters of God born not of blood, nor the will of the flesh but of God".

The natural Human Identity

The natural person (not yet born again) in the word of God, is revealed as still in darkness he has not yet passed from death to life and from darkness to light (Colossians 1:13). The natural person is still not born-again, he is governed by Satan through sin in his dead spirit (Ephesians 2:1), his mind and his physical senses are also enslaved by the enemy to rebellion and disobedience. The book of Genesis reveals to us how God defines death. When Adam disobeyed God, he was still alive – his body did not drop dead on the ground, and the LORD God told him that from the day he eats from the tree of the knowledge of good and evil he shall surely die, and indeed Adam was a dead man walking, so then what died in Adam? it was his spirit, (Genesis 2:17). Spiritual death means to be separated from God, then physical death is when the body returns to the dust, and the separation of the spirit and the body (see John 19:30). Eternal death or what the bible calls the second death, refers to being eternally separated from God and this only happens when one does not accept Jesus Christ as Lord and saviour of their life (see John 14:6 Revelation 20:11-14). Adam's spiritual death resulted in humankind being separated from God spiritually (Romans 6:23). In Adam humanity died spiritually and Satan ruled them through sin, death, fear, poverty and disease; it took nine hundred and thirty years for sin to kill Adam in the natural (Romans 5:12). The bible says, "For the wages of sin is death but the gift of God is eternal life through Christ Jesus" (Romans 6:23). The natural man cannot know God without the new birth experience through receiving the Lord Jesus as Lord and saviour, (Romans 10:9). He is a slave to Satan through sin, poverty, sickness and disease and the only hope he has is Jesus Christ who is the way, the truth and the life. (1 Cor. 2:14), "The natural man does not receive the things of the Spirit for they are foolish unto him." Spiritual things to the natural human do not make sense as he only lives in the sense realm, which means the evidence to a fallen human is always **sight**, **logic** and **experience**. And all of these evidences have some truth in them, yet they should not be used as the means to seek and know God for the Lord is bigger and greater than sight, logic and experience. The fallen human has traded faith for fear, sonship for slavery, assurance for doubts, health for sickness, life for death, prosperity for poverty, freedom for condemnation, truth for lies, love for hate, unity for disunity appreciation for ungratefulness. These were the unconscious and unintentional agreements Adam and Eve made when they believed the lies of Satan and traded with him, but praise be to God that in Jesus Christ there is hope for the natural human.

The carnal human identity

The carnal human is the one who has been born again, but has not yet matured in the knowledge of who he is in Christ. In first Corinthians chapter three we see Paul addressing the church of Corinth as carnal, which sounded pretty harsh for the church that flowed so strongly in the gifts of the Holy-Spirit, and yet they were still carnal and flesh dominated (1 Cor. 3:1). It is possible to flow in the spiritual gifts and still be carnal and flesh minded. Many Christians today get confused when they see a brother or a sister being used mightily by God and the next thing they see is them still having problems with envy, jealousy and pride issues, and would wonder how could this be, but the answer is simply a lack of spiritual maturity. Being gifted is not a substitute for character. Spiritual maturity comes through spiritual growth in the word of God and the carnal human is still governed by sense knowledge, which in its nature is trusting in human strength, works and human performance (Galatians 3:10-13). The church of Corinth had moral problems and challenges, and Paul never addressed them as people who had lost their salvation and as wicked, but rather he expounded to them their identity as believers not to walk as carnal people but to be spiritually minded, to be aware, and conscious of the new nature they have received in Christ. (1 Cor. 3:1) (2 Cor. 5:17). Today in the church the challenge for many believers is what the Corinthian church faced; many Christians do struggle with addictions, mental oppressions and fear because they still walk in the carnal nature. But they are still believers who have not become aware of their new nature and privileges they have as the word of God reveals through the power of the Holy-Spirit (John 8:31-32). The difference between the natural and the carnal person is that, the natural person is not yet born-again, is still spiritually dead and the carnal person is a born-again believer who is either a babe in Christ (1 Cor. 3:1) or walking in the carnality of his mind, still full of envy, strife and division. A carnal person yields to the flesh and does not submit to the Holy Spirit. Romans 8:6-7 shows that to be carnal minded is death; the carnal person is limited in their senses, and lives life through their own strength, still walking in ignorance and blindness of their physical senses. On the contrast, the word says that we walk by faith, trusting the Lord that all things work together for our good because of His faithfulness (28).

The spiritual human identity

The spiritual human is the one who has fully grown into the understanding of righteousness in Christ (2 Cor. 5:21), he or she walks by faith not determining their circumstances of life by sight but by faith in the word of God because of full trust and dependency on God's faithfulness. A spiritual human allows the Holy-Spirit to govern, lead and guide them through the word of God (Matthew 4:4) (Proverbs 3:5-6). The strongest aspect of the spiritual human is their love walk; the word says that perfect love cast out fear, because fear has to do with torment and judgement. The spiritual man/woman walks in their new creation nature which is identical with Christ. This nature is not earthly, neither carnal but spiritual, thus possessing all the qualities of God in the inner person who knows that they are freed from all powers of darkness through Jesus Christ. The moment we become born again, the same life that was in Christ that enabled Him to walk in power and victory we receive, live and walk by. I remember at some point in my journey with the Lord when I began to focus with strong emphasis on how God sees me and therefore I studied the letters of the Apostles, specifically the letters of Apostle

Paul. I began to notice that some of the challenges I faced with condemnation, guilt and fear in my walk with the Lord were just results of me not being aware and conscious of being the righteousness of God and the way the Father sees me being exactly how He sees Jesus (1 John 4:17). I then began to spend most of my time renewing my mind in the word and confessed all the times what the word of God revealed about me including the promises of God. Most of what ministers preach and teach about repentance, is to do with renouncing secrets, sins and habitual life style of addictions a believer faces in their walk of faith, yet the word repentance has nothing to do with the above primarily. The word repentance simply means to go back to God's perspective returning to the original way God thinks and see things from that view point (Isaiah 55:8-11). It is not a message for addressing people's behaviours but a constant thing that needs to be consistent in a believer's life through the renewing of the mind. Repentance occurs every time the word of God is preached, and therefore repentance takes place because the word brings transformation. Without repentance people remain locked in the carnality of their thinking; having a renewed mind is not about whether you make it to heaven or not, but simply how much of heaven you want to manifest in your life now. True repentance starts within by being awakened to your identity in Christ. (Hebrews 4:12). The spiritual person is not dominated by the flesh or the carnal nature for he or she walks and is led by the Spirit of God (Galatians 5:18) and is under the New Covenant established on better promises (Hebrews 8:6).

Meditating on God's word

Throughout history scientists, psychologists and philosophers have spent and still do spend millions and even billions of dollars on the development of the soul and intellect of man and body and yet have never discovered the mystery of the human spirit. We have gyms to develop our strengths, schools, colleges and universities to develop our minds but never for once has humanity seen the importance of our spiritual growth. This can be described in my own terms as the unequal balance the body being dominant, the soul being in control and the spirit being made powerless due to lack of it being developed through the word of God (Luke 1:80). We need to understand that just as the human body can be developed to become stronger, so in the same way the human spirit can be developed to become dominant over the soul and the body. Here I will share on meditation as a key to developing your spirit. Also it is the key to hearing the voice of God, walking in the spirit and being obedient to the Holy Spirit. As we develop our spiritual life, we will never walk in confusion and wrong places because we become aware of God's perfect will which enables our decision-making to become sharper and accurate. Your spirit has knowledge beyond the physical world and therefore these are the benefits of building your spirit being. Many Christians have been born-again for years and even decades but they still have not grown spiritually which is why some of them are still subject to sickness, fear, poverty and the oppression of the enemy because they are not living from the spirit being. When we rightly divide humankind, it becomes the key to victorious Christian living, and through the bible the word of God makes it clear that humankind is a spirit being, with a soul that lives in a body and it is through our spirit God intended us to live, therefore our soul and body must subject to our spirit if we are to walk strong spiritually.

To develop the inner person, **feeding and meditating on the word of God,** is the first thing (Matthew 4:4). When we feed on the word of God we will never become hungry spiritually because it is the manna of a believer – the bread of God unto us. Our spiritual mouth that we feed through is called **faith;** without it you cannot feed your spirit. Meditation and feeding on the word of God must be daily through faith, for meditating on the word without faith is like feeding your spirit with your mouth closed. Faith is one of the key ways believers build their spiritual life as faith makes the word a revelation to the spirit. To meditate is to go over something again and again until it is digested into small tiny particles. A good example of this in a negative sense would be worrying. Whenever someone is worried or anxious they are meditating and going deeper into their problem through thinking over it constantly until it grows into fear. This is described as the law of consciousness; it means that whatever you are conscious of and think about daily you attract upon your life and will eventually become a reality because that is what you believe. Suppose you constantly think about how difficult life is; sooner or later your body will accept what your mind keeps telling you and begin to work on an action plan to fulfil the thoughts you have been dwelling on. Therefore, many people lose determination and passion in life because they believe that no matter what they do they cannot progress in life. The root issue started with what they have been thinking and meditating over the years about themselves until it became a belief system and mindset they live by. The point is people already practice meditation without being aware of it, but I want to emphasise God's way about meditation. The word of God instructs us to meditate day and night in the word so that we shall bear fruits in all seasons of our lives and that whatever we **do** prospers (Psalm 1:2-3). When we meditate on the word we position ourselves to bring God's insight and foresight into every matter we face daily. Isaiah describes this concept in a beautiful way declaring that His ways are not our ways and His thoughts are not our thoughts (Isaiah 55:8-11). As we meditate on the word of God two things happen; first our spirit is fed and secondly our mind is renewed to think and act like God. To meditate God's way firstly we have to be well acquainted with God's promises concerning all matters of life in His word and then choose to accept what He says as ultimate truth. An example can be dealing with worries. The word of God in Philippians 4:6-8 gives instructions about what to do when worries confront you. It says. "Be anxious for nothing but in all things, gives thank unto God". When you meditate on that, worries will no longer disturb your peace because you will always be trusting in God for everything.

Chapter 4
God's image and likeness

Worship is intimacy with God that causes His likeness to rub off on us, and through this constant experience we grow in knowing the nature and the ways of our father God (Psalm 103:7). To many Christians worship has become an experience that's only encountered during a corporate gathering within a church service which is not wrong but there is much more to it than just singing songs during a service. In Genesis, we see God creating humankind in His image and likeness – the image speaks of His abilities. Adam had the same abilities and demonstrated in the garden this ability by naming all the animals in chapter two of Genesis. In all aspects we can see humanity as ambassadors of God. Despite Adam bearing the image of God, the likeness of God grew in him as he constantly fellowshipped with his heavenly Father. The Lord visited Adam in the cool of the day constantly to fellowship with him. That was the way Adam knew more about God. There was no bible printed; it was in his heart and his daily experience with the Lord. If you notice the word Yahweh which is the word LORD in most English translation, its first mention is in Genesis chapter two. The word Yahweh reveals who He is as a covenant keeping God and relational God, who seeks fellowship with His creation. In saying that, I am not referring to creatures, animals and plants but rather humankind. One of the elements of worship is to know the Father through consistent union that birth an inward revelation of him (Genesis 1:27). Adam was created in the image of God and the likeness was not mentioned in verse 27 but in verse 26 of Genesis chapter one; "God said, 'Let us make man in our image and likeness'". Many people do not notice that in the creation of humankind the likeness is not mentioned (Genesis 1:27). The reason is because likeness can only come through intimacy and relationship. Just as in the natural, a child naturally carries the image of the father because of the DNA, but the child might grow up and behave not like the father. Because likeness is built through relationship, communion and constant fellowship, likeness is always attached to deep intimacy and fellowship. The Hebrew word for father is **Abba** which literally means God is the spiritual leader of the house; the house here is a **person** who is the temple of the Spirit of God. (Genesis 1:26) God had two aspects to creating humankind; first His image and second His likeness. Then again we see in verse 27 that only one is mentioned and that is image not likeness. The enemy knew if he could destroy Adam and Eve's fellowship with God, humankind would be dead spiritually but would still carry the image of God and function, but the likeness of God wouldn't be in them, because it's cultivated through fellowship by spending time to know Him and that is why God visited Adam in the cool of the day.

Intimacy the key to worship

Growing up as a young person in the charismatic and Pentecostal circles I have heard many statements about worship which puzzled me. One example was being created to worship, and there were many more. As a young believer, I struggled to understand the purpose of worship because it was always emphasised without accurate insight of God's purpose, and it seemed like God demanded worship before He could do anything. Going to conferences and revival meetings the same statement of, "You were created to worship" loops around. This caused me to go in a journey of discovering the original intent of God in regards to worship. What I want to unfold here is not to create a theological debate on worship but rather seeing the heart of the Father through His word and to unveil His original purpose for humankind in relation to worship. The original purpose of God creating human beings in Genesis was for them to have dominion, rulership fellowship with Him. Today many people within the body of Christ use worship as an element of begging God due to the lack of revelation knowledge concerning God's purpose in regards to worship (Matthew 8:1-2NKJV). "When He had come down from the mountain, great multitudes followed him. 2 And behold, a leper came and worshipped him, saying, 'Lord, if you are willing, you can make me clean'." The leprous man here in the word can represent today's different mindsets people carry in their approach to the Father. His approach to Jesus reveals that he suffered for many years from rejection, identity, fear; he was a man that was in total pain looking for an answer. According to the law of Moses when someone had leprosy they were classified as unclean and an outcast of the society and they would be cast away from the society and live alone. So you could imagine what life means for this leprous man; he lived alone without anyone coming close to him or even visiting to see how he was doing. His mind frame was puzzled about how Jesus would respond to him; when he was sitting down planning to ask Him for his healing, his natural instinctive expectation was for Jesus to say "No" to him because he could have seen himself unworthy, rightfully deserving the leprosy as a form of punishment. The scripture tells us that he came and worshipped Jesus saying "Lord if you are willing you can make me clean." What I want to point out here is the question he asked, because it reveals the desperation of his life and condition. This leprous man could have had many thoughts running in his mind at that time that were opposite the heart of God. His question reveals that he didn't have the understanding that God is good and that is His nature and that it is His will that all should be healed delivered and saved; perhaps his condition of leprosy made him view Jesus as distant from him. If you read the gospels clearly you will notice that the leprous man was the only person who asked Jesus if he was willing to heal him. Under the new covenant we are not beggars but sons and daughters of God; we don't approach the Father anymore with any sense of guilt, distance or fear but we have the right to boldly come before the throne of grace and commune with our heavenly Father. This leprous man speaks prophetically of the concept many have in regards to worship. Many have made worship a ritual centred around worship songs, worship nights rather than an expression of the spirit to the father, worship is deep calling out to deep. Worship is inbuilt in humankind to relate to their heavenly Father. True worship is all about intimacy not begging. In these last days, the Lord is releasing an increase of the original purpose of kingdom worship. Worshippers are not only pastors, leaders and the band, but rather every believer is a worshipper. When we understand this simple truth, we transform the atmosphere around us because His presence is being released through us. This is what worship does; it stirs His presence and increases the awareness of who He is as our heavenly father, and cultivates the lifestyle of a worshipper in these last days.

Chapter 5
What is a Kingdom?

Without understanding the concept of what a kingdom is, the message of the bible becomes impossible to understand. The reason is because the purpose of God creating humankind was to establish and expand His kingdom through them on earth. Adam was a royal agent carrying the image and the likeness of God with a kingdom mandate to align earth to heaven and to be a king over God's creation. The fall of Adam led human beings over many years to lose the understanding of the true philosophy of a kingdom, adapting to the style of modern government concepts, such as democracy, communism, dictatorships and socialism and all these styles of government have produced more confusion and chaos. Humans made kingdoms in the past and now have not grasped the true understanding of a kingdom and the ideologies of a monarchy and royalty. History has proven that the concept of a kingdom to humanity has always been designed for one family to have power above all people resulting in injustice (sometimes!), atrocities and oppression over the citizens. What makes the kingdom of God different from all kingdoms is that it is the only kingdom that makes all citizens relatives of the King Jesus and kings themselves. The bible is a book about a king and a kingdom. The concept of God concerning a kingdom is the true prototype of a government established on His faithfulness and righteousness; every kingdom and government on earth has always made an attempt to imitate the perfect kingdom of God structure. Democracy, dictatorships, communism and socialism have been human ways and attempts to reach the standard of the kingdom of God without the most important person on earth, the Holy Spirit. Jesus was sent to come and restore what Adam lost. He is the restorer of the kingdom; His death and resurrection established the kingdom government on earth and gave humankind the right and rulership as kings and queens. Adam did not lose a religion, but a kingdom. The redemptive work of Jesus Christ is based on this purpose. Jesus came to re-establish the kingdom. Let's look at components of a kingdom to have a better understanding of the kingdom based on Jesus Christ's kingdom message and concept. All kingdoms have these concepts:

1. **A King and Lord**
   The king is the representative and embodiment of the kingdom; the authority that comes down from the words of the king is final. Jesus is our king and He also made us kings to rule and reign with Him – such a great privilege (Revelation 1:6NKJV).

2. **A territory, domain**
   The domain is where the king exercises his authority, the earth is the Lord's but He gave dominion and stewardship to humankind to rule and look after His creation (Psalms 8:4-6 24:1NKJV).

3. **A constitution, the legal structure of a kingdom**
   The constitution is what gives the kingdom legal structure, it contains legislations, policies, laws of the kingdom. The bible is the constitution of the kingdom of God. It carries the concepts of God concerning everything He wants His citizens to know. The bible contains the will, purpose, plans, promises, privileges and rights God has for His citizens.

4. **Citizens of the kingdom**
   The citizens in a kingdom are the people who are governed by the king; only citizens of a kingdom can inherit the benefits of the kingdom. The safety and welfare of the citizens is provided by the King; the lifestyle of the citizens will be reflected by the King's welfare. As citizens in the kingdom, God has promised us, His children, all things we need for life. God plans has always been for His sons and daughters to possess the earth (Matthew 6:33NKJV).

5. **Regulations and policies**
   The laws in a kingdom bring discipline and order. Unlike democracy which the citizens do make the laws and rules. Everyone in the kingdom including foreigners are to obey the laws of the kingdom; the words of the King are basically the laws of the kingdom. Jesus is our perfect King. He does not oppress His citizens but rules them with love and righteousness.

6. **Privileges, rights and benefits**
   In a kingdom, you have privileges that the King gives every citizen. These privileges are part of the package of being a citizen.

7. **Conducts and ethics – the culture and lifestyle of the kingdom**
   Every kingdom has ethics, standards, morals and a way citizens live, it is what forms their culture. In the kingdom of God we are called to be light and agents of change in every area the Lord send us.

8. **The defence force, social security and army**
   The army in every kingdom provides safety and security to the citizens of the kingdom. In our modern democratic government it is called a defence force. In a kingdom, citizens don't fight to enjoy the privileges of being protected by the army. In the kingdom of God, He has given his angels to serve us; the believers are citizens of the kingdom (Psalms 78:49-50 103:20-21) (Matthew 13:40-42).

9. **A commonwealth, economic**
   In a kingdom, the commonwealth is the economic system which gives all citizens the same rights and privileges to access wealth and financial security. God has promised to meet all the needs of his people according to His riches in glory, not according to their circumstances and challenges (Luke 12:31-32).

10. **The kingdom culture**
    The culture of every kingdom is reflected by the King's nature. The kingdom of God is the only kingdom whereby the King Jesus Christ serves and calls His citizens brethren. In the kingdom of God, all citizens serve one another and love one another because that is the nature of the great King Jesus.

The Kingdom mandate

The Kingdom is given unto us who belong to the family of God (John 1:12); it's a Kingdom of sonship, power and dominion. The moment Christ enters your life and becomes your Lord and saviour you are no longer a slave but a son or daughter in the kingdom. There's a completely changed identity you receive, and you become a new creation with a higher life. I call this "kingdom lifestyle" whereby you are in charge over all things God created (Psalm 8:6). This position puts you over sin, sickness, poverty, fear, failure and destruction. Our present assignment in the kingdom as sons and daughters of God is to release the father mandate here in our communities, market-place, nations and cities until it aligns with the will, plan and purpose of the father. There are many believers who are in the Kingdom but still have a slave mentality because they have not yet discovered their identity, the plans, purpose of God and their present assignment in the Kingdom. One of the misconceptions about the kingdom of God that Christians seem to carry, is that one day when Jesus returns then we will have the power to make the difference in this world. This mentality leads many Christians to just sit back and become complacent thinking about leaving the earth and going to heaven either through death or rapture. The great commission is the greatest mission given on earth; the church of Jesus Christ is responsible to bring change and transformation to the entire world. God's plan for redeeming mankind and the earth back to Himself is assigned to the church. He has called us into His kingdom to expand it to the uttermost ends of the earth (Matthew 24:14). This misconception came as a result of religion. Man's traditions and customs about the Kingdom of God pass down from many generations due to lack of revelation and teaching concerning the kingdom of God. The original plan of the father choosing to expand His kingdom through humankind is not a response to the fall of humanity but it has always been an eternal purpose in His mind. Earth is a colony of heaven; a believer is a kingdom ambassador carrying a heavenly mandate in the mind of the father. Humankind is to be on earth as God is in heaven exercising dominion; this is a marvellous and fascinating truth. The resurrection of Jesus Christ is the receipt of the kingdom being restored back to humankind. Jesus is exalted in three dimensions; heaven, earth and hell with all power and authority having been given unto him. The part that many miss out on is so simple but yet powerful that if Christ is the head of all things and He is seated at the right hand of the Father signifying rest and victory over all His enemies and we are His body, that means we are also seated with Him and His victory and triumph is ours, and all things are also under our feet. This is the truth many believers do not see (see Ephesians 1:17-21 Philippians 2:5-11). The kingdom is experienced and expanded through the resurrection power of Jesus; the resurrection of Jesus Christ is the greatest demonstration of power in the history of creation (Colossians 1:19). When God created humankind, He designed and shaped him for dominion and rulership just like Himself. In the Old Testament we see the shadow of the Kingdom of God in the nation of Israel; the Old Testament is a shadow of what was to come. In the Old Covenant Christ is concealed and in the New Covenant He is revealed. We belong to a triumphant kingdom; every believer has to awake to the reality of this truth and live it. The kingdom is advancing through sons and daughters who have caught the vision of the Father; creation eagerly awaits for the manifestations of the sons and daughters of God who will stand up to declare and demonstrate the power of the everlasting and unshakeable kingdom. In the book of Daniel

(11:32) the word of God reveals the key to doing great and mighty exploits is knowing your God. Doing is always a reflection of being; to know the heart of the Father is the key to knowing your identity. The more we see the father in the person of the son Jesus, we become transformed from glory to glory through beholding His face; in fact the word "face" in the Hebrew means personality, features or even favour of the person being revealed to you. We should always seek the face of the father (2 Cor. 3:17). Our lives have to constantly reflect His image and likeness. Only sons and daughters have access to kingdom heritage for they have matured from infancy of childhood. One of the main reasons why it seems like the kingdom is not expanding is because there are too many baby Christians within the body lacking the revelation of sonship, spiritual heritage, legal rights and kingdom authority. Jesus was born as a child but was given unto us as a son; the difference between a child and a son is that a child has little difference to a slave or servant because they lack understanding of what they have and who they are because of the infancy of the mind – limitation to know the truth about their identity and heritage. On the other hand, sonship in the kingdom is all about maturity. Jesus was always aware of His sonship and that was the key for Him as King. He knew who He was that is why He needed no approval from man to tell him who He is. True sons are marked with confidence and boldness; they fear nothing, they are full of the Holy-Ghost, and walk in the anointing and power. Romans 14:17, "For the kingdom of God is not eating and drinking, but righteousness and peace and joy in the Holy Spirit." The context of this scripture is about the conscience and how we shouldn't pass judgement on another and become a stumbling block, but I want us to see another angle which is an attribute of the Kingdom. The Kingdom of God is not a physical kingdom, it's spiritual in its nature but manifest in the natural realm through the power of the Holy-Spirit in sharing the gospel and revealing the King Jesus. And of course I don't dispute that one day there will be a physical manifestation of the kingdom; when King Jesus returns in glory that will come. Many have been taught a lot about eschatology which simply means end time studies, without accurate insight about the present assignment God has given to his church to restore the kingdom on earth as it is in heaven, destroying all the works of the devil over continents, nations, cities, states, suburbs and villages. This ignorance of the present assignment of the church has led many Christians to park on the rapture bus stop waiting day and night for Jesus to come because they just want to escape the issues of life. They are not aware that His divine power has given all we need for life and godliness through the virtue of our knowledge in the finished works of Jesus Christ. The church has to be illuminated with abundance of revelation knowledge of what God did in Christ in order to enjoy all the privileges of the kingdom here on earth (Matthew 4:23 2Corinthians 5:17-21). Jesus in His earthly ministry demonstrated the power of the kingdom when He taught and preached the word; signs, wonders and miracles would follow him naturally, to confirm His message about the kingdom of God. Another fascinating angle to look at is found in Luke 17:22 where it speaks about the kingdom being within us. It unveils a wonderful truth about us being the ark or the dwelling place by which the King of kings expands His kingdom through the earth realm. In the spirit world, spirit cannot function on earth without a body and that is why Satan used the body of a snake to get to Adam and Eve to sin against God (see Genesis 3:1). In the same way God has to dwell on the inside of us through his Holy Spirit to expand His kingdom. That's the first thing He did when Jesus finished His assignment – He sent the Holy Spirit. This is an amazing

What is a Kingdom?

truth; we carry the presence of the great King on the inside and He wants to expand His reign by using us. Jesus told the Pharisees that the kingdom of God doesn't come through careful observation, nor will they say, "see here" or "see there". The mistake or the ignorance of the Pharisees was, they always did not want to believe that the kingdom of God had come when Jesus ministered healing to the sick, setting the captives free, casting out evil spirits and taught the life of the supernatural kingdom (Mark 3:1-5). The natural human mindset has no understanding of the things of the spirit "for they are foolishness unto him." When a person walks by sight and follows their senses they will always miss out on what God is doing in the now. As I have said earlier, many Christians are parked on the rapture bus stop always singing songs about "One day I will be successful, happy, completely healed when Jesus comes back," not knowing that Jesus already defeated Satan and his principalities, and has given us all authority over all powers in hell, earth, and heaven. NOW is the time to rule and reign over the enemy because we are kingdom citizens and ambassadors.

Releasing the Kingdom and His will in prayer

Matthew 6:9-10 "In this manner therefore pray; 'Our father in heaven, hallowed be your name. Your kingdom come, your will be done on earth as it is in heaven'." The Lord Jesus here is teaching His disciples how to pray. We can learn some principles in His teachings about how His will (heaven) is released on earth through prayer. Apostolic prayer is all about the King's domain invading the earth. Jesus the High Priest and the Apostle of the Father has already paved the way for us to continue expanding the kingdom here on earth. Prayer is reinforcing the victory of Jesus Christ over the enemy by agreeing with heaven. In Amos 3:7 there is a wonderful truth. It says that the sovereign Lord does nothing unless he first reveals to His servants the Prophets. We are living in the times where the Lord is filling the earth with the knowledge of His glory, will, purpose, timing and kingdom strategies. Prayer is the key to this increase of revelations of divine mysteries of His kingdom expanding here on earth through the church (Ephesians 3:9-11). The life and the ministry of Christ was backed up with great demonstration and manifestation of the Kingdom realities through miracles, signs and wonders, and He taught a new way of living the kingdom lifestyle that even a teacher of the law by the name of Nicodemus acknowledged that no one could do unless God is with them (Acts 10:38). So what made the ministry of Jesus so powerful that His disciples picked it up from His life? Luke 11:1 reveals the disciples realised that Jesus spent most of His time talking to the father more than talking to humans. So they asked Him, "Lord teach us how to pray." They discovered the key to why Jesus could do mighty works, and it was prayer. They saw how accurately Jesus was doing what the Father had assigned Him in every situation without any distraction. Prayer brings the counsel of the Father to your present situation and condition. Jesus walked in the perfect will of God. He never did things without directions from the Holy Spirit. This is all a result of a prayerful life. Remember that on many occasions in the gospels Jesus doesn't pray much for people's problems, rather He always responded to their needs that, "According to your faith it shall be done" or He would give thanks to His Father instead of asking Him to do something (Matthew 8:1-8). This intimacy is only birthed through prayer. Jesus knew His oneness with the Father so much that He stated that "The son can't do anything without the Father; the son can only do what He sees the father doing for it's the father working in Him and through Him" (John 5:19 14:10-11). Jesus never had any sense of doubt and unbelief in His life and ministry in regards to any situations that ever faced

Him (John 11:41). This was the secret His disciples discovered, and they wanted to know how to pray and see the same results as Jesus and become like Him. This is powerful. When we pray that His kingdom come on earth as it is in heaven and His will be done on earth as it is in heaven, we are releasing His heart beat, mind, will and purpose to our lives, families, communities, nations, governments, economy, and politics. God wants to raise people who can pray His heart-beat. One of the things the Lord is releasing in these last days is the spirit of prayer and intercession over the church because there are so many promises and prophetic words that need to be birthed through prayer. We see in the life of the early church how prayer plays a strong role in walking in the purpose and will of God. Apostle Peter was locked up in prison (Acts 12:1-15) but as the church lifted her voice in prayer God delivered Peter supernaturally. The Lord is calling His people to a deep place of intimacy where He can reveal the mysteries of the kingdom over nations, cities, kingdoms and people for this end time harvest. When we pray, we enter into a legal agreement with His will and purpose being established here on earth. Secondly we download His prophetic strategies and mysteries of releasing His will through the church. Thirdly we are setting the captives free through intercession on behalf of the unsaved and lost and binding every force of darkness that's at work against the purpose of God. Lastly prayer brings **revelation**, **elevation** and **manifestation** of the purpose and will of God.

Mental battle

Throughout history psychologists have done numerous experiments on the power of a conditioned mind to show the effects of what a controlled and programmed mind thinks like. I heard a story once of a goat which the owner tied down for few weeks and after the period of that time the goat became so conditioned that after it was freed it couldn't notice the difference between being free and being still bound because its mind was so conditioned and programmed to think being bound was the new normal. The owner tried all means to make the goat realise that he was free but still the freedom could not go through the goat's mind, so he decided to just pick him up and carried him home. This is what happens when we develop wrong mindsets and belief systems. It becomes difficult to change, receive and learn new things from the Lord because a conditioned mind has already been programmed to think and believe in a certain way. A good example in the word of God can be seen in the lives of the children of Israel. It was easier for God to deliver them from the power of Pharaoh, than from the power of their own thinking. It took 40 years for them to enter the promise land because of their wrong thinking which created doubts and unbelief in their hearts towards the promise of God (Numbers 14:11). The way of the wilderness was used by God to untrain them from all the years of being programmed to become slaves internally which is the result of external slavery, and prepare them for their prophetic destiny which was Canaan. One of the things God wanted to make sure that didn't happen was for the children of Israel to enter the promise land with the condition of a slave mentality of Egypt, because this would mean that they came out of Egypt but the ways, thinking patterns of Egypt still remaining in them. It would also mean that they were delivered but not freed because freedom requires one to think independently and become responsible and accountable over their life. This is more work than slavery, and this seemed hard to the Israelites who were once enslaved because being a slave had benefits, such as having free food, free houses, showers and water to drink. Even though it wasn't first class, they settled for it. This is one of the fruits of a slave mentality; it conditions people to go for second best rather than aim for first. It also makes

What is a Kingdom? 49

people live as survivors rather than thrivers and a successful achiever. Secondly a slave mentality views poverty as a normal thing and that wealth and riches aren't for everyone. Without a mental transformation the actions we take to change will only produce a new location, but you still act in your old ways. This is basically what happened to the children of Israel in a nutshell. Later on I will expound more on how we can renew our minds to understand His will for our lives, families, business, work, ministry, nations and cities. Slavery isn't a location but a mindset one is conditioned in, and programmed to think about who they are not, what they don't have, what they can't do, and where they can't go. That's why you find many people around in our world today saying statements such as, "Be realistic, the struggle is real", because their mentality has been conditioned and programmed to a limit where they can't proceed. This thinking is the result of a slave mentality inherited through sin from Adam, but the good news is that through Jesus Christ we have a new mind (2Corinthians 2:16) (2 Timothy 1:7). God's word speaks many times about the importance of being careful what we allow our mind to think about; our thought patterns will reveal who we are. "As a man thinks in his heart so is he". Our minds have to be constantly renewed and after they're renewed we will experience the transformation in our life style (Philippians 4:8).

Repentance is more than changing behaviours and responding to altar calls

To many Christians, especially Pentecostals and Charismatics, the word "repentance" has been thoroughly abused and used in wrong contexts that even the original meaning and intent of it has been thrown out of the window. The word has left many with the impression of changing conducts or a response to altar calls at church. Growing up in church I have always thought of the word "repentance" negatively because of how it was used. Every time I heard that word, I had a notion that it was always about renouncing secret sins or something bad you did, but I came to realise that many people who took the definition of repentance had a change of conduct and behaviour only to go back to their previous lifestyle after realising that it wasn't a transformation of the heart and mind. True repentance is heart and mind first, then behaviours become the fruits of a transformed heart and mind. Just to clarify something here before I proceed. The point I want to address isn't to start a theological debate on where you stand on the definition of this word, rather we want look at the definition from the contexts of the ministry of Jesus and the origin of the word. The word "repent" is the Greek word metanoia, which means to "change your mind," "change the inner man in relation to accepting the will of God in exchange for yours," it also can mean a total U-turn. The English word is repent – a compound word, the first part re- means going back to the original state of something where it began, the second part there is pent- which means first or top from the word penthouse – the top of a high-rise building. Repentance is not just a shallow message focused on people's behaviours but it's returning our mind, heart and actions to God. Therefore, the original intention of the father is for us to have dominion, rulership, to multiply, to be fruitful and to duplicate His kingdom on earth. Humans are gods on earth as God is in heaven (Genesis 1:26-28). In Matthew 4:17 repentance is not just behavioural change, but the state of your spirit being redeemed, altered through the renewing of the mind by the word of God. Saul who later became one of the greatest Apostles of the Lord Jesus was a man lost in darkness, being ignorant thinking that by prosecuting and killing the believers he was doing God a favour. He was a very zealous man after the things of God but he never understood and knew who Jesus was because he never had an encounter with Him. On his way to Damascus he had an encounter with the Lord and his life was completely turned around forever. For three days he was blind signifying that a blind heart and mind will never see and know the Father. Saul was blind but he never knew; he thought all his good deeds pleased God. After the three days of being blind, he was led by the Lord to a man named Ananias who prayed for his sight to be restored back completely. The name Ananias means "the grace of God" which signifies that repentance is an act of God's grace through changing our hearts and minds from the blindness and ignorance that leads us to dead religious works based on performance rather than faith. Constant repentance will increase your faith level to believe God and His promises and it's also a medicine for doubts and unbelief.

Understanding His will

The will of God is vital for every believer to understand because in the mind of God it's no longer up to God for us to live a better life, but it's up to us to know and apply what He has already done for us through His son Jesus. The best life has been given but the choice is up to us. Every believer has been enthroned to rule and reign with Jesus. It's called the triumphant life; as sons and daughters in the Kingdom your life should never be in confusion because you are equipped and built for success and victory. It's in your DNA - wherever you enter you possess (Joshua 1:3). The first thing I will deal with before proceeding forward about the phases of God's will, is to expound on some reasons why many don't walk in the perfect will of God. Many times we hear phrases from Christians such as, "I have received so many prophetic words and promises from the Lord and I haven't seen one fulfilled yet", being ignorant that personal prophecies are conditional and they never fulfil themselves. It takes work, yeah WORK. Throughout the entire bible, individuals have missed walking in the perfect will of God due to preconceived ideas of what they thought about the will of God for them, and this led them to follow their senses and plans (Proverbs 3:5 19:21), rather than being led by the Spirit of God. Preconceived ideas are results of our past mentality, and lies of the enemy we believe. Preconception is basically us taking the word God has spoken and trying to help Him fulfil it through our own ways. We see this in the life of Abraham when he began to look at his age and began to panic and question God's method of fulfilling His promise of a child for him and Sarah. Due to preconceptions mixed with doubts, Abraham then decided to help God with his own idea which was that Hagar could be whom God meant for the promise to be fulfilled and he was clearly aware of the fact that God told him his wife Sarah would have a son in her old age. The significant insight here is we can't walk in the perfect will of God with a servant mentality, a mindset that tries to earn what has been given by God's grace. I want to expound furthermore here on the different **phases of God's will**. In Romans 12:2 the word of God lists three levels to God's will as we continue to renew our minds in His word. The first phase is listed as the **good will of God.** In this phase we see many living their lives, including believers. It is the stage where people are comfortable with human achievements, accomplishments and then define that as a fulfilled life, not being aware that's the perfect will of God for everyone. Living in the good will of God is not the promise of God for His children but many choose to stay and park themselves there as their final destination. God's promises are clear and specific; He has promised to all who believe in His son Jesus, not just eternal life but abundant life where we get the concept of what is called "Zoey" life or another term is the God-kind of life. The word "Zoey" means God's self-existence life; this life isn't just length but quality. Through the life of Jesus, we see Him living this kind of life. Many think it is only when we get to heaven that we will live the perfect will of God. That kind of thinking is very religious and deadly; it was the same mentality the Israelites had on their journey to the promised land; they were freed physically but still had slave mindsets, (Exodus 14). After they crossed the Red Sea they began to complain about simple things of life such as food and water when they had already witnessed the power of God and being delivered supernaturally from Egypt. This goes to show that until we understand and change our thinking and accept that God never intended humans to live in heaven but on earth, we will always push our present rights, benefits and blessings to heaven while God wants us to enjoy them here on earth. The nation of Israel is a warning and an example for us not to miss out on what belongs to us due to being ignorant and disobedient to the promises of God. Jesus demonstrated that we can bring heaven to earth through the revelation of who we are in Him. The Zoey life produces in us divine health, wealth, wisdom, prosperity and the joy of the Lord. Jesus, the perfect example, was not just comfortable with the good will of the father but He walked in the perfect will of His father in total submission fearing nothing. In these last days, the Lord is doing a great transition where there's an increased revelation of His perfect will in the body of Christ. For so many years the church has been bound by religious spirits, teachings and mentality to always push the promises of God about living in His perfect will as something we will one day experience when Jesus returns. But Jesus already gave us power and authority to rule and reign here on earth as it is in heaven, for in the mind of God we are kingdom ambassadors on an assignment to align earth to heaven in every aspect; this is the purpose of The Great Commission. The second phase of the will of God is the **acceptable or the permissible will of God**. One of the greatest gifts God ever gave humanity is free will, but it's also very dangerous. Due to free will, people have inherited promises and blessings of God, but also many have missed God's promises, blessings and plans due to not choosing to follow the directions and the instructions of God. We will study this in the life of two characters in the word of God which are Saul and David. Free will reveals love. God gave Adam and Eve free will for Him to prove He truly loved them, because without free will there will be no accountability. Free will is good, but how we use it is what makes the difference. In the book of 1st Samuel chapter 8 we discover how Saul became the king of Israel. The people came complaining to the prophet Samuel with an agenda of having their own king because they wanted to be like other nations. It was comparison and competition that birthed the leadership of king Saul. This was not God's plan, because the nation of Israel wanted to copy other nations' governmental systems not knowing all those times in the past God had been their King. The reason why many Christians aren't walking in the perfect will of God but in the good and permissible will of God, is because they follow patterns set by others and they try to mimic other people's process but they end up being an echo not a voice. I call it operating under borrowed anointing and destinies. This concept has caused many to become what I call human parrots of other people destinies and callings. The prophet Samuel tried to convince the people not to go ahead with the agenda of choosing their own king, but they insisted until God intervened and spoke to Samuel and told him that the people weren't rejecting Samuel but Himself. This is a such a powerful statement for God to say something like that; it clearly reveals that it was not the time yet for Israel to have their own king. When we read a few chapters ahead we see Saul being anointed as the king of Israel; he was the choice of humans not God. We should understand that despite Saul's kingship being a result of the permissible will of God, he was still used by God but it wasn't smooth for 40 years. Israel suffered under the leadership of Saul. The permissible will of God is Him allowing you to live life as you desire based on your free will, God will never force His perfect will on you; it is a choice individuals make on their own. **The last phase of God's will, is the perfect will of God.** To live a complete fulfilled life we must understand the term and meaning of the **perfect will of God.** Firstly, His perfect will is not living life without challenges, problems, trials or any obstacles. Christ Himself faced many challenges (see Hebrews 2:18) but He still completed all the Father commissioned Him to do. The perfect will of God is fulfilling the purpose of God for your life. It's living within the range of every good promises your heavenly father has given you (see Ephesians 1:3). David was a great example of this. He was anointed King by the prophet Samuel but it took him thirteen years before he walked in the fulfillment of his purpose and assignment. The Lord trained David for thirteen years behind the scenes, and no one knew him yet. David learnt how to kill Goliath in the secret place of training while he was a shepherd boy. God used the environment around him to prepare him for his prophetic destiny as the future deliverer and king of Israel; he had to fight and kill lions and bears to protect his father's sheep. When God prepares you for His perfect will He does it in silence. The Lord will always set you apart from everyone to prepare, teach you principles and establish you for His perfect will. It took Jesus thirty years of preparation before starting His assignment on earth. He was in the secret place being groomed and trained by the father to fulfil His purpose of saving and redeeming humankind from the powers of darkness (see John 5:19-20). Walking in the perfect will of God requires you to know your spiritual assignment. We live in a physical world but we carry a spiritual assignment. The kingdom is within us the children of God through the Holy Spirit. We are called to infiltrate our environment and sphere of influence with the kingdom of God that's our spiritual assignment. Every region Jesus went to in the gospels, he took the good news of the kingdom of God and demonstrated it through teaching, preaching and healing the sick; the end results were cities, towns and villages and people being delivered and transformed in all aspects. Spiritual warfare is part of the assignment. This does not mean we are fighting to victory but rather from victory. Our fight is against all the combatants of darkness that are against humanity. Part of our assignment is to stand in the gap and be intercessors for our families, friends, nations, and government that the kingdom of God should invade them. The fight is called the good fight of faith. God has given us weapons beyond deadly. We are to expand the boundaries of the kingdom of God into dark areas. The enemy has bound people through witchcraft, religion, poverty, fear, violence and spiritual bondages, and set the captives free through the authority given unto us in the name Jesus.

Chapter 6
The Great commission

The great commission has always been perceived by the church as an **evangelistic** mandate, which is not wrong but rather it is an Apostolic mission primarily of God's kingdom invading the earth though the church. This is not implying the idea of everyone being an Apostle to be part of the great commission, but simply to be apostolic in nature, thinking about **duplication** of heaven on earth. God's ruling, thinking, purpose and will invading the earth through the church. The word Apostle means *sent one, messenger, ambassador, representative, missionary or someone sent with a specific message, instruction, mission and assignment to a region.* The great commission goes beyond just winning souls for the Lord; it's all about duplicating His world in the earth through the revelation of his Kingdom on earth as it is in heaven. The way to enter the kingdom is called "repentance" and it is to do with a change of heart and entering a new of way of thinking and living. The scriptures in the gospel of John 18:36 makes it clear that the Kingdom of God is not of this world that's why when Jesus was asked, about claiming to be a King, He responded, "My kingdom is not of this world". This then gives us the understanding of what Jesus means when he responded to the Pharisees when He was asked concerning the kingdom, His answer was that the Kingdom of God is within you. The great commission carries principles we can learn and apply as apostolic people. The first principle is GO (see Matthew 28:18-19). Jesus said "Go into all the world starting from Jerusalem, Judea, Samaria and to ends of the earth". The going principle is all about evangelism – sharing the good news of the kingdom about the love of God revealed in His son, starting from your family, friends, relatives and strangers. When this message is shared, it produces salvation, restoration and deliverance. The gospel of Jesus Christ is power of God unto salvation (Romans 1:16-17). The second principle is the MAKING OF DISCIPLES, the great commission is about making disciples who will implement and live the word of God as reality. Discipleship is all about training, equipping, teaching the Christian to be firm and matured in the Lord and to become effective in the kingdom. Discipleship is the core of the Christian victorious walk. In the book of Acts chapter nine we learn a powerful lesson about what a disciple can do in the Kingdom. A disciple by the name of Ananias was instructed by the Lord in a vision to go and minister healing to Saul who later became one of the greatest Apostles who wrote a third of the epistles. Ananias was not a Prophet or an Apostle but he was just a disciple who understood that when you have Jesus in your life you are anointed to do the same works He did, and even greater, for He has promised that greater works shall be done by those who believe in Him. Discipleship activates the believer to become active and responsive to be a participator in the kingdom. Lack of discipleship in the body of Christ has created bystanders and spectating Christians who just attend church but do not understand their purpose in the body of Christ. Through discipleship comes an understanding of your purpose as a Christian, the journey of a Christian and many vital tools that will establish your faith on solid ground with Jesus Christ our foundation.

The third principle is BAPTISM. The fourth principle is TEACHING; the word is profitable for teaching, instruction, correction, training and wisdom. The church now needs revelatory teaching ministries that will unveil the identity of the believer like never before. Teaching ministry brings foundation and spiritual maturity. Many Christians don't know much about who they are in Christ and what they have in Christ, and it causes them to walk in defeat and lack. In these times God is pouring out revelation knowledge upon His children abundantly because there is work to be done.

Understanding Jesus' purpose and assignment

Hebrews 3:1 reveals to us that Jesus is an Apostle, the sent one of the father with an assignment of redeeming humankind from the dominion of Satan through death, fear, sickness, disease and poverty. In the gospel of **John 8:23-29,** Jesus goes into depth with this concept of being the sent one. In His constant dialogue with Jewish people He kept stating that He only does what His father sent him do. Jesus was sent by the Father with an assignment of redemption. He never lost sight of it because the mission was established in His heart. He knew and understood the purpose for which He was sent (see John 12:27-29). This Apostolic commission of making disciples of all nations was hidden in Christ until after His resurrection from the dead. In the scriptures in Matthew chapter four when Jesus was in the wilderness during His fast for forty days and forty nights being tempted by Satan, the enemy came and tempted Him with the kingdoms of the world. I would like to pose a rhetorical question here; who gave Satan the kingdoms of the world or authority to rule in this earth realm? When you reflect on this question it reveals what happened to Adam and Eve when they yielded to temptation of the crafty serpent, the Devil. Adam lost dominion over the earth the moment he ate from the forbidden tree of the knowledge of good and evil. He and Eve became slaves to Satan through sin, death, poverty, sickness and disease. Since the fall of Adam and Eve, humankind has been under the oppression of Satan for thousands of years, teaching them destruction, death, fear, false identities and poverty, or you could say sin put humankind in to self-destruction mode where they are disconnected from their redeemer God. The absence of God's ruling and presence is to invite chaos and destruction into our lives. Adam lost his given right and authority to rule and reign as a god on earth to Satan through sin. Satan knew if humans were against God they would be separated from God and would lose all rights and privileges. Jesus was sent by the father to restore humanity to the original plan of God through redemption (see Romans 5:12-18). His Apostolic work is evident in His ministry. Jesus went about teaching and preaching about the kingdom of God; He revealed and demonstrated the heart of the father to humankind (John 1:1-14 3:16), He is the word become flesh, the love of the father in action. His life reveals the thoughts and intentions of the father in action. He is the image of the invisible God. In Jesus, we see the embodiment of the Father. His language reveals the language of God to humanity, His unconditional compassion and love reveals the unconditional compassion and love that the Father has towards humanity. On the cross He took our place that through His death, burial and resurrection we become the righteousness of God and He was raised through the power of the Holy Spirit for our justification as our High Priest to mediate heaven and earth through His precious blood. I call

The Great commission

it the divine exchange. He took our place that we might take His place. He took our infirmities, disease, shame, condemnation and judgement so that we are judged righteous through His blood by the Father. He loved us even though we denied Him and turned our backs against Him. His resurrection is the greatest demonstration of power in the entire history of mankind; He rose as King of Kings and Lord of lords holding in His hands the keys of death and hades. He has overcome and conquered Satan, sin and spiritual death. Therefore, He was exalted by God the father who gave Him a name that is above every name that at the mention of the name of Jesus Christ every knee bows and every tongue confesses that Jesus Christ is Lord to the glory of God the Father. He is our true model of the great commission for in Him we see the blue print of the father on how to draw humankind to Himself.

On Earth as it's in Heaven discovering his world

Let's go on a discovery here to unveil what His **world looks like** so that we can have a better understanding of what we are commissioned to do. Romans 8:19NKJV, "For the earnest expectation of creation eagerly waits for the revealing of the sons of God". The whole creation including nature, animals and humanity waits for the manifestation of the sons of God, to bring a transformation and a greater change that will be a revolution in the history of humankind. (Romans 4:17). This scripture unveils the prophetic aspects of God for He calls those things that are not as though they are. In the natural when things look negative it's impossible to paint a positive picture, but God works the other way around. He sees beyond the natural and releases what is in the spirit to the natural circumstances. When Abraham and Sarah were barren God never saw them barren He always saw them with Isaac. I know this might surprise some people, but

God never created humankind to be barren. The first blessing He spoke to man was to "Be fruitful and to multiply". The mind of God only contains plans and purposes related to His will. Our present circumstances do not change the perspective of God in relation to His promises and plans towards us, for He has set the end from the beginning. This means that all things shall work together for your good. When you peel onions for long you start dropping tears but that does not mean you are crying because something bad happened to you. So it is the same with how you view your circumstances. No matter how ugly things look God will turn it around for your good. It might have been a difficult season of life; the devil might have attacked you but God will turn that pain into gain. The first key to discovering His world and releasing it on earth as it is in heaven is the **key of faith** (Hebrews 11:3-6). God unveils the nature of faith in creation. He spoke all things into existence except humankind. What we can learn here is that faith is creative, which means our God is a creative God; His world is unlimited – it's the realm where there are no impossibilities, (Exodus 4:15-16). One of the most remarkable events in the bible where we see God demonstrating this nature of faith is in the book of Exodus. During the journey of the Israelites to the promised land, the Lord spoke to Moses to stretch his rod out towards the Red Sea, and as Moses obeyed Him, the Red Sea parted and there was dry ground in the midst of sea in the natural. That is impossible but with God all things are possible. The faith of God is releasing the invisible into visible. Further in the gospels in the ministry and the life of the Lord Jesus our true blue-print of His world, we learn and see the importance of looking at things through the eyes of faith, (Mark 9:23). The supernatural was natural in the life of Jesus. It was bread and butter for Him to demonstrate that every child of God is a walking wonder, full of the glory of God. Many have this excuse in their mind that Jesus did all the miracles, signs and wonders because He was God in flesh. Yes Jesus is God manifested in flesh, but He grew as man, He grew in wisdom and in knowledge and had to depend on the Holy Spirit just like anyone. The bible says in Hebrews that He was tempted in all areas yet without sin, (Hebrews 5:18) (Philippians 2:8-10). Through the word we understand we can't please God without faith and also salvation is impossible without having faith in Jesus Christ. In the book of Hebrews (11:6) the scriptures reveals that without faith it's impossible to please God. The word **without** comes from the Greek word *choris* - it describes the idea of being outside a specific location. A good example is real estate; if you live close to the city your property will be costly due to it being close to many privileges. But if you live far from the city the value of the house becomes cheap. The word "without" unveils the key to growing in faith. The point here is that faith has location and that location is the word of God. The closer you stick to the word of God the more faith grows in you to see His world as your world like Jesus, but if you take the word casually your faith in the word will be casual not firm and steady. God is pleased when we enjoy what He has done for us through faith. When we give maximum attention to the word of God we will experience maximum miracles and results in our lives.

The second key to discovering His world is His **word**, (2Timothy 3:16), "All scriptures are inspired by God through the power of the Holy-Spirit". The word reveals all about our beautiful heavenly Father, through Jesus Christ the living word of God. Every thought to the details of who God is are revealed. He is the mind of God in action. The word is so powerful - it reveals and teaches us what the Father thinks about us, the plans and thoughts He has towards us (Psalms 8:6) (Psalms 23:1-6) (Genesis 1:28). Through knowing and understanding His word by the revelation of the Holy-Spirit, a believer has a greater access to bringing His world here on earth (Proverbs 25:2). The word of God is a treasure chest full of great mysteries, blessings, wisdom and inheritance. The wise saying of Solomon gives us a glimpse when he said it's the glory of a God to conceal a matter but the glory of a king to search it out a matter. There is a wonderful truth here we can learn; when we spend time studying and reading the word of God, He begins to give us keys of revelation knowledge to access what belongs to us, our inheritance, His wisdom blessings, etc. Ignorance and lack of knowledge are the two underestimated diseases the enemy uses to cripple many believers today from accessing the supernatural realm that rightfully belongs to them (Isaiah 5:13). Isaiah reveals that through lack of knowledge people go into captivity; being in captivity is to be bound, not walking in the spirit of wisdom and revelation. Many, including believers, have accepted a defeated lifestyle because of being ignorant to the truth of the word of God about their victory over sin, death, sickness, disease, fear and poverty. The scriptures say "Be transformed by the renewing of your mind that you may know and approve the perfect will of God". The transformation only happens as our thinking is washed by the word of God and begins to transfer the thoughts of the Father into our minds. The Greek word for **word** is *"logos"* which literally means a *thought being expressed through words*. The word of God is the thought of God. When we take God's words and put them into our minds we begin to think, believe and act like God in all areas and that's what Jesus demonstrated because He was the logos of God who became flesh. Through Him we see all the components of the father's thoughts towards humanity in action. We are the reflections of our thought life. Proverbs 23:7, "As a man think in his heart so is he". At many times it's not what you are that holds you back rather, it's what you think you are not. It was easier for God to deliver the Israelites from the power of Pharaoh than from the power of their own thinking. We need to renew our minds constantly with revelation knowledge concerning His will purpose and plans for our lives and to know the direction to take (Isaiah 55:8). Isaiah was right by saying God's ways aren't like our ways and neither His thoughts like our thoughts. Then He goes to say "As the heavens are higher than the earth so are His ways to our ways and our thoughts to His thoughts". The high thoughts of God aren't hidden in heaven but rather in His word (Psalms 119:130). As we seek His word we begin to think like Him; His revelation knowledge gets to be transferred into our hearts. This will cause our ways to be like His ways. The steps of the righteous are ordered by the Lord, (Psalms 103:7), God made His ways known to Moses and His acts to the children of Israel.

The third key is the **Holy Spirit**. When we become aware of who lives on the inside of us we become bold and supernatural. The Holy Spirit is the most important person on the earth realm and we need Him more than ever before. Part of the ministry of the Holy Spirit is to reveal to us the mysteries hidden in Christ Jesus. Throughout the whole bible we see the Spirit of God coming upon individuals whom He anointed at certain times to prophesy events that would take place within the course of time. The Holy Spirit revealed the birth of Jesus through many prophets in the Old Testament. The Holy Spirit is not only known as the Spirit of truth but He is also the Spirit of wisdom and revelation for He brings the counsel and the mind of God unto us concerning all matters; He is the mighty counsellor.

Chapter 7
The power of the gospel

The bad news got here first that is why when the pure gospel based on the finished work of Jesus is preached with the resurrection power and demonstration, it sounds too good to be true. Today we hardly hear the pure gospel of our Lord Jesus Christ preached with the focus on Him alone because it has always been mixed with legalism, religion and traditions of humans. The question to ask is "If the gospel is pure good news why are the majority of Christians projecting depression, fear, failures, doubts and familiarity?" as though it is something valueless, second hand and cheap. Jesus paid on the cross our complete salvation package; He bore our iniquities, transgressions, disease and poverty so that we live an abundant life in Him through being recipients of His finished work through faith. Many within the body of Christ have not yet truly understood the message of the gospel of Jesus Christ; they have cliches and assumptions in their mind about it. The message of the gospel is the power of God unto salvation. When the gospel of God's grace is preached to unbelievers it releases the same power that raised Jesus from the dead into them and this is what produces salvation and transformation from a life of oppression to a life of promotion. The gospel carries the power to resurrect every dead thing within humankind. When Apostle Paul was ministering in Lystra (see Acts 14) he preached the gospel and it created faith in a man who was born crippled. The faith in the crippled man was produced by the message he heard Paul preached. I believe he heard Paul preaching about healing and that God wanted him to be healed and free from the infirmity he suffered. When the crippled man realised that he did not have to live in the oppression again, Paul saw the faith in him to get up and walk. He commanded him to walk and so he leaped and started to walk. It was an instant miracle through the power of the gospel. Faith comes by constant hearing of the word of God. It produces assurance and captures the invisible as visible and God is good and He will keep every promise He made in his word. The second prophetic insight we can learn about the power of the gospel. The story of the crippled man healed in Acts 14 is that humans without Jesus are spiritually crippled and paralysed and it takes the power of the gospel to bring healing and deliverance from this spiritual infirmity. The doctor will fix the body but the Holy Spirit through the gospel heals spirit, soul and body. That is why Jesus is the greatest physician that ever lived. He cured humanity from a spiritual infirmity that no doctor can solve. Wherever the Apostles went and preached the gospel, lives were transformed (Acts 2:38-41). At the first sermon Peter preached, 3,000 people were saved. This must be the good news because it's never happened before. The only reference in the Old Testament under the law is 3,000 people died at the foot of the Mount Sinai when they disobeyed the Lord which goes to show that there is no good news in the Mosaic covenant. The Mosaic covenant was actually only for Moses and the Israelites (see Exodus 34:27). Today we are under a New Covenant based on better promises (see Hebrews 8:6) (see Galatians 3:19-25). Through Jesus the perfect man who fully satisfied the wrath of God (see Romans 3:21-26), today God the Father sees humanity through His son Jesus Christ. This is the gospel; it's all about unveiling the wonderful works of our Lord Jesus through understanding His death, burial resurrection and ascension. Jesus on the cross was our substitute; He died not for us but *as* us. Reading Romans chapter five we understand the bible says that sin entered the world through one man Adam, and through sin, death came which was spiritual death, then came sickness and disease, poverty, fear, condemnation and physical death. Then it goes to say that just as in the same way sin entered the world through one man, how much more shall we be justified by the blood of the Son of God Jesus Christ and by Him through His obedient reign in life abundantly. The power of the gospel is unveiled and unleashed when Jesus is the central focus because He is the good news. Through Him all humans have access to the father (see John 14:6). To explain the gospel in illustrative language, it's like a child of a King lost from a young age, who grew up without his identity of royalty and heritage. And through these false identities and the rise of low esteem in him, he then decides to go on the streets and live as a beggar, because it's the only way he views the solution to his life. But one day the king finally decides to visit the streets dressed in casual clothing just like the civilians, to look for his lost son. He continues to walk on the streets and comes across a young beggar that resembles him, so then he stops to find out about him. Through questioning his background, the king fully realises that he has found his son who he lost, he then redeems him from the life of poverty and begging and takes him home to his palace where he really belonged. Through Jesus we have been redeemed from spiritual

The power of the gospel 69

bankruptcy being slaves to the devil, but because God is so rich in mercy He delivered us from the kingdom of darkness and took us into His kingdom where we are kings and priests through blood of His son Jesus.

The four views of redemption

In my early walk with the Lord before I received the revelation of righteousness by faith in Christ, I struggled within with sin consciousness; at some point I even doubted my salvation because of the legalistic sermons which I had heard during my early walk as a new believer. Those times I was not enjoying my salvation but rather I was enduring it. In this world a human being has access to three main voices. There are many voices we hear in day to day life, but what I mean specifically is that humankind has three main voices that influence their choices and decision making; the voice of God, the voice of human's consciousness and the voice of Satan. In the Garden of Eden before the fall, Adam and Eve were only conscious of the voice of the Lord. They knew nothing about sin consciousness because their focus and awareness was on the presence of the Lord, but the moment they fell, the word reveals (Genesis 3) that Adam and Eve became conscious of their nakedness and three instant manifestations were seen in them; **fear, shame** and **guilt** (see Genesis 3:9). Notice it was not Satan who told them they were naked if you read the texts carefully. Adam had no clue of who he was after the fall; his senses became dominant and the soul component – will, emotions, personality and mind dethroned the spirit and Satan became his master through sin. Everything Adam did from that moment forward came from sight not faith, fear not love. The first fruit of sin consciousness is self-righteousness which is the mask of a broken man on the inside (see Isaiah 64:6). The other two voices humankind can listen to, are the voice of God through his Spirit and the voice of the enemy (John 16:13). Jesus said, "My sheep know my voice". He is implying here there is certain indication of identifying His voice, He is the good shepherd, His voice is peaceful, gentle and He always leads by His word. Lastly the voice of the enemy. It's very clear to know the voice of the enemy because the word calls him the accuser of the brethren (Revelation 12:10). His voice carries condemnation, deception, lies and destruction (John 8:44). We are made righteous through the blood of Jesus. This has nothing to do with merit but purely faith in the perfect and eternal blood of Jesus (Hebrews 10:8-10). Righteousness is a gift of God unto humans broken on the inside seeking a relationship with the Father. Many have tried to reach God through good deeds and many of these good deeds are not necessarily bad, but they are not the means to become righteous. It is by faith alone in Jesus Christ. Righteousness can be imputed unto us (see 2 Cor. 5:21). To understand righteousness more effectively let us break down what happened on the cross. Firstly the Father was working in Christ and not on Christ because Christ did not need redemption, but the work was for us (John 3:16).

The first assignment of Jesus on the cross was His **substitution work.** He took our place and we took His place which means He who knew no sin became sin so that in Him we become the righteousness of God. At many times we try to use logic to understand how can that be possible when the scriptures say all things are possible with God (see Luke 1:37). Remember in Adam all became sinners through the act of one man, Why? Because through Adam we were born so we are part of him. So what he did effected all humankind. Adam's decision affected all humanity because we were in him. A good example of this is if your parents were from Australia and your mum is pregnant with you and you were born in Alaska will you be identified as an Australian or American? The answer would simply be you will be an American so the point is that the decision of Adam affected everyone. We were not born in the condition Adam was created in, but we were born in the condition Adam passed on through sin. The substitution work is not God punishing His son Jesus, but rather He gave His own life for us to save us all from sin, sickness, death, fear and poverty. The Old Testament reveals types and shadows which are hidden mysteries and truths of Jesus' substitution work. Jesus became the sin offering. The scapegoat in the book of Leviticus is a prophetic picture of Jesus who became our scapegoat from sin, death, sickness and disease and fear (see Leviticus 6:27-30). He could not die if sin was not imputed into Him and he became our scapegoat when He took our sin upon Himself. He was separated from the father so that we can be accepted by the father (see Leviticus 16:5-7,10).

The second part of Jesus' assignment I call it **redemption view** (1John 3:8). Jesus was sent by the Father to come and destroy all the works of the devil. The word "destroyed" in verse eight of 1 John comes from the Greek word **Luo.** It's also the same word found in the gospel of John (11:44) when Jesus raised Lazarus from the dead. This word describes the idea of unwrapping something that has been wrapped with a cloth or even ropes, so the redemptive view is Jesus freeing us from all the chains, ropes of oppressions and bondages we were bound with by the enemy. When we understand the redemptive work of Jesus on the cross we will know exactly what belongs to us. The revelation knowledge of what happened from the cross to the throne is key for every believer to be triumphant over the enemy. Through the redemptive work of Jesus Christ, we have been given authority and power to access and possess all things that belongs to us (see Romans 8:28). We were bought with a price, the blood of Jesus, child of God. Your life is not cheap; it cost Jesus His life. A divine exchange took place on the cross.

The third assignment of Jesus' redemptive work on the cross is to establish a New Covenant, (**covenant view**) (see Hebrews 9-10). God under the New Covenant has cut an eternal covenant with His son Jesus and through Him we have become partakers of this covenant which is based on better promises, (see Hebrews 8-6,7). The new covenant is established on the finished work of Jesus on the cross of Calvary. Every believer is given a legal invitation to be the beneficiary and recipient of this covenant and its benefits which is good news. The Old Covenant is focused on "You shall not" because it was a covenant based on works and conditions; your blessing and prosperity are conditional (see Deuteronomy 28). Under the New Covenant the focus has changed. It is no longer about our faithfulness, effort, will, power to earn His blessings and please Him but rather His faithfulness to keep His word, and bless us unconditionally. In the New Covenant, the Lord is the initiator. He is the one that leads us and keep us through His Spirit. We no longer carry the spirit of an orphan and slavery, but we call Him Father, a word that was rarely used in the Old Covenant because there was no revelation of the fatherhood of God. Through Jesus Christ we have been engrafted back into the family of God by shedding of His blood on the cross of Calvary. His blood is the foundation of the New Covenant.

The eternal Blood

In the olden days, the most usual covenant practiced among cultures was always the blood covenant where two people come into an agreement of shedding blood through cutting their wrists or even animals being cut into halves symbolising two people becoming one by dying to themselves and forming one new person. It was a common practice among Hebrews and many nations even till today. Some cultures still practice this kind of covenant ritual. Under the Old Testament the blood of bulls and goats were used as means of atonement but they only covered sin for a year but did not remove sin. The scriptures make it clear that if the blood of bulls and goats would have brought remission of sin and forgiveness then the High Priest would not go yearly to the Most Holy Place to give constant sacrifice for the remission of sin for the entire nation of Israel (see Hebrews 10:1-4). Yearly the high priest had to go into the most holy place with the blood of an animal which had to be accepted by God. Sometimes if the blood of the animal is not accepted for a year the whole nation of Israel experienced a terrible and painful year of no rest or prosperity because they became exposed to the enemy without a covering from God. The blood of bulls and goats only reminded the people of sin because it only covers it but does not wash it away from the heart. The Mosaic sacrificial system was a shadow of the good things to come. It was a mystery that contained the assignment of the Messiah Jesus who was to come and give His life as the precious lamb of God who takes away the sin of the world. Jesus came to establish a better covenant not based on the blood of animals and human works. It is a covenant that no longer requires you to sacrifice the blood of animals for His blood is so powerful that it does not cover sin but it removes and washes sin and destroys the power of the devil over your life; this is the gospel. The blood of Jesus redeems us from sin, death, sickness, disease, fear, poverty and from all the powers of darkness (see Colossians 1:12-13). Through the blood of Jesus we have legal rights as sons and daughters of God in the kingdom; we are no longer slaves but have become part of the royal family where we carry the name above all names. The blood gives access to covenant promises concerning all things. God has promised us there are about 32,000 promises in the bible concerning everything the Father has in store for you. Through the blood of Jesus you are a victor, overcomer, more than a conqueror and a champion. The blood of Jesus is our receipt that we show condemnation, guilt, shame and the attacks of the enemy that we are overcomers. The blood speaks of better things; it speaks forgiveness, love, grace, righteousness, new creation and faith.

9 steps of Hebraic and ancient rituals of making covenant

- **STEP 1.** Take off the coat or robe (see 1 Samuel 18: 1-4) the coat represents the person, giving your all to another and vice versa
- **STEP 2.** Take off belt (see 1 Samuel 18: 1-4) the belt represents strength, giving your strength
- **STEP 3.** Cut the covenant (see Genesis 15:1-9 Jeremiah 34: 18-19) giving your life, to start a new life
- **STEP 4.** Raise the right arm and mix blood (see Isaiah 62:8) becoming one through an eternal covenant
- **STEP 5.** Exchange names (see Genesis 17:5-15 32:18) taking the last name signifying a new family
- **STEP 6.** Make a scar (Isaiah 49:16) the scar represents memorial
- **STEP 7.** Covenant terms (see Genesis 31: 52-53 Joshua 9) possession becomes equally divided
- **STEP 8.** Eat a memorial meal (Genesis 26:28-30 31:44-54) covenant celebration
- **STEP 9.** Plant a memorial tree (see Genesis 21:27-33 31:44-54) testimony

The difference between a contract and a covenant

Contract

A written or spoken agreement, esp. one concerning employment, sales, or contract, which is intended to be enforceable by law.

An agreement with specific terms between two or more persons or entities in which there is a promise to do something in return for a valuable benefit known as consideration. Conditions apply at the Centre of it.

Covenant

A covenant is an agreement between two people that becomes one through shedding of the blood. Unconditional once it's sealed with an oath, quite frankly the term covenant is costly because it's all about sacrifice and love; grace and oneness are the Centre of a covenant.

The fourth assignment of Jesus' redemptive work on the cross is called the **moral view**, (see John 3:16 and Romans 3:23-25). The moral view is all about the righteousness of God. Many people always wonder why God did not use other means to save humankind. The reason is that God is faithful and He works according to His word. When He created humankind, He gave him dominion over the earth which means if anything happens to humans the only way He can rescue them will be through an invitation because He gave human beings free will to invite or not invite Him. Prayer is simply humans giving God legal access to work on earth through Him. Throughout the whole bible God's agenda has always been to partner with humans to accomplish His purposes. This is because without human beings God will not, and without God human beings cannot. God has the power but on earth human beings have the authority and God will not use His sovereign power as an excuse to do whatever He wants to do because He is a faithful and just. God only works according to his word. The bible is a book that reveals the love of God and His search for individuals that will allow Him to work through them to destroy the works of devil. He used young and old, male and female to demonstrate His love and righteousness but humankind were not fit for the job to bring redemption from the power of Satan. So He decided to come down from heaven taking a form of humanity and lived among us for 33 years experiencing all the challenges humankind went through including being rejected yet without sin. Therefore, He took upon Himself all our sins that we may take His place and become what He always desired us to be and that is our relationship being restored as sons and daughters not slaves of the devil, sin, fear, death, sickness, condemnation and poverty. Jesus Christ's death, burial resurrection and ascension are the demonstration of the righteousness and justice of God. The heart of the father was unveiled in the death of His son Jesus Christ. He gave His only begotten son as our ransom so that we can be delivered and redeemed; He legally justified us through the blood of His son Jesus. In Christ Jesus, you see all the attributes of our heavenly father; that He loves you, and has forgiven you. All you should do is to come to Him through Jesus Christ, the righteousness of God who is our advocate that defeated our adversary the Devil through His blood, and freed us from the dominion of sin and Satan (see Romans 6:23).

When we study the gospels carefully we will see two important views about the redemptive work of Jesus Christ. Firstly, the human's perspective from the account of Matthew, Mark, Luke and John. They wrote what they witnessed about Jesus being inspired by the Holy Spirit. On the other hand, through the writings of Apostle Paul we see the X-ray of what took place on the cross from the perspective of heaven through the revelation of the Holy Spirit (see Galatians 1:1-2). These two views reveal the human's perspective and God's perspective; the journey of the believer is to focus on what God saw through redemptive work of His son Jesus. In the mind of the Father, everything God did in Christ He did for us as though we did it and we are given all the credit for His finished work. On the cross God was working in Christ not on Christ because His resurrection was not for Him but for us; His immortality, is our immortality, His victory is our victory (see 2 Cor. 5:19) (see 1 John 4:17). Paul reveals that the revelation of Christ is too deep beyond comprehension, and that he still wanted to know more about what happened from the cross to the throne.

The fruits of our righteousness in Christ

- **Our position is restored**, fearlessness before the Father
- **Communion is restored,** no sense of guilt and condemnation
- **Faith is restored,** faith in His word becomes natural as a baby breastfeeding from a mother
- **Peace is restored,** oneness with the Father (see Ephesians 2:14)
- **Liberty is restored,** (see Ephesians 4:5-7)
- **Sonship is given,** (see John 1:12)

The mystery of the Gospel in the life of Abraham

Many Christians don't realise and capture this wonderful truth concerning the gospel as glad tidings, (see Luke 2:9-10). The gospel is all about the wonderful news of our Lord Jesus Christ and His redemptive work which He did for us on the cross. Not only did He die but He rose in victory and He is seated as King of Kings and Lord of Lords at the right hand of the Father. This mystery of the gospel was firstly revealed to Abraham when he had an encounter with Yahweh, the covenant keeping God (see Genesis 12:3). The Lord spoke to Abraham and told him that in him all the nations shall be blessed. Abraham did not only hear the message but he believed it was credited to him as righteousness. Galatians 3:9NKJV, "So then those who are of faith are blessed with believing Abraham". Another wonderful example to look at in the New Testament is the story of Mary the mother of the Lord Jesus, and Zachariah the father of John the Baptist. The Angel Gabriel appeared to both of them and simply proclaimed to them glad tidings (see Luke 1:13-18-31-38). The Angel Gabriel first appeared to Zechariah and had a dialogue with him and he told him glad tidings that he would have a child with his wife Elizabeth even in their old age. But he struggled to believe the word of the Angel of the Lord. Just immediately after that Angel Gabriel visited Mary and told her that she had found favour in the eyes of the Lord and she would conceive and bring forth a son and He shall be called Jesus. Mary believed the glad tidings and replied to Angel Gabriel "Let it be done according to your word". She didn't use her logic to understand how would it happen but she simply believed. On the other hand Zechariah struggled to believe because he tried to reason out how would it happened since he and his wife were old. The point here is that faith to experience God's grace and goodness is birthed through believing the good news He has revealed through His son Jesus Christ. Both Zechariah and Mary heard the glad tidings but both of them had different experiences; Zechariah was mute until his son John was born. The prophetic insight we can learn from Zechariah and Mary is that for us to experience the goodness of the Lord He must mute our unbelief and doubts to silence because His word is true. When unbelief and doubts are muted they have no effect and power to hinder His blessings and promises concerning our lives. Unbelief must be muted in all areas of life to experience all the promises of God. Today many believers still struggle to believe this wonderful news of redemption, salvation, freedom through the gospel. When the angel appeared at the time Jesus was born the first thing the angel of the Lord proclaimed was "Fear not" then stated, "For behold I bring you good tidings of great joy which will be to all people". This was the fulfilment of the promise God gave to Abraham in Genesis 12:3. Abraham lived a blessed life though he did not live to see the day the Messiah was born physically but he saw in the spirit (see John 8:53-54). The power of the gospel was evident in the life of Abraham because he believed what God said and the manifestation rained upon his life abundantly, (see Genesis 13:2). The gospel of Jesus Christ is the power of God unto salvation, wealth, health and good relationship. Before Abraham encountered Yahweh, he did not even have a clue what the gospel was. He was just a man broken; even though he had a heritage of wealth already, he knew something was missing. Bible scholars make it clear that the background of Abraham was paganist. Abraham was an idol worshipper before he encountered the living God. We can look at this stage of Abraham's life as the stage we are in before new birth. We were lost in darkness worshipping all sorts of idols in hope to find the living God and that is exactly what Abraham did. The gospel revealed to Abraham firstly the love of God for him and the great plans He had for him. God showed Abraham that He had a great plan for him and that stirred faith in him and he was obedient to the voice of God. Notice in verse one of chapter 12 it says, "The Lord had **said** to Abram ". I highlight this to show the importance of how faith comes by hearing only not seeing because faith originates from the spoken word of God (see Romans 10:7). Abraham believed the gospel and he was saved. Remember the gospel is not just the first four books of the New Testament but rather the good news revealed through them. Abraham experienced this powerful truth even before the four gospels were written. The gospel also activated the inheritance God gave to Abraham. God promised Abraham a land which was to flow with milk and honey. Later his descendants possessed the land the Lord promised him. This prophetically speaks of abundance God has for His sons and daughters. Today we are living in that promise of abundant grace God promised Abraham (see Genesis 13:14-17).

Chapter 8
Salvation the seal of dominion

Salvation is not an escape route to heaven but rather a seal of dominion for every child of God on earth over all things Adam lost authority over, through Jesus Christ. It is fascinating when you discover the amount of Christians waiting for the rapture to happen because they are tired of painful life experiences. Some even have changed their prayer to only be "even so come Lord Jesus come" instead of agreeing with God so that His will be done on earth as it is in heaven. The moment Jesus said on the cross "It's finished" Satan was stripped of all his armour and was defeated once and for all, (see Colossians 2:15) (see Ephesians 1:19-23). All things have been put under the feet of Jesus and we are part of His body the church. We rule and reign with Him as kings and priests. To have a better understanding of this the gospel of Matthew chapter four gives us a wonderful insight. When Satan tempted Jesus with the kingdoms of this world and their glory the condition was for Jesus to worship him (see Matthew 4:8-10). Jesus rebuked him with the word of God and stood His ground. The focal point here is that a temptation cannot be something you already have. If that is the case it would not qualify to be even a temptation (see James 1:14). One of the primary assignments the Father sent Jesus for was to legally restore the earth back to humankind because Adam lost dominion and authority over the earth and he became a slave to Satan through sin, death, disease and poverty. So Satan knew legally the earth belonged to him before Jesus legally defeated him. He tempted Jesus because he knew Jesus came for the restoration of man's authority over the earth and as well, to destroy all his works (see 1 John 3:8). God gave Adam authority over the earth not heaven; this is where many miss it. Adam fell short of the glory of God, not fell from heaven, that is the difference. The plan of God since creation for humankind is to rule and be God's representative on earth and that has not changed despite the fall of Adam.

Kingdom Ambassadors

The day we enter the kingdom of our heavenly father we become citizens and ambassadors of the kingdom with a specific mission to infiltrate the world with Kingdom message, culture and mindset. The kingdom mandate is for the earth to align with heaven's agenda. God gave human beings stewardship over the earth not ownership. The moment Adam and Eve thought they could do anything they wanted without accountability to God they immediately lost the garden. The principle we can learn here is that the earth and its fullness belong to the Lord but He gave it to humanity to manage and be a steward of His wonderful creation (Psalms 8:4-8 24:1NKJV). The word ambassador carries the idea of a diplomat of the highest rank sent by a King, president or a country to be a representative in the nation and colony they are sent to. This means they are sent with a specific mission and purpose to represent the interest and policies of their kingdom, nation and country here on earth. We are citizens and ambassadors of the kingdom, assigned with a special task. In every generation, kingdom ambassadors are history makers not history readers. During the Roman kingdom era, the Romans had the best concept of expanding their kingdom empire; other kingdoms before the Romans era had different concepts of colonisation. Slavery and exploitation were the main methods used before the Romans empire era and this involved killing all men and leaving children, women, and mothers. They would uproot them from their land and take them back to their kingdom and make them slaves. This concept of colonisation did not work as effectively as the Roman concept of colonisation. The Romans had a prototype of the kingdom of God government style; their idea of slavery was psychological and systematic. They would influence other nations with their culture, language, lifestyle and thinking. They understood that these strategies are keys to effectively have colonial power over different nations that were part of the Roman empire. As ambassadors of Christ God has given a mandate to change our world and bring His style of leadership and government to the earth. We are to bring a shift in the political, economy, family, education and other areas of the society. The Holy Spirit is senior advisor on bringing this change child of God. The Father sees you as His great diplomat and agent of change. This is your mission here on earth. You don't have study politics and international relations but simply you are qualified by your heavenly Father to be an ambassador in every area He sends you. Change is not coming from heaven but is in the action you take in being obedient to the instructions of the Holy Spirit.

In the Kingdom, you are an ambassador who walks by faith not by sight. You initiate change and make things happen through His grace.

The battle beyond Pharaoh

The nation of Israel spent 40 years wandering in the desert, in a journey that could have taken a few days from Egypt to the promised land. Their exodus from Egypt was the easy part but for Egypt to come out of them it took forty years and only two people made it to the promised land with the younger generation: Joshua and Caleb. The older generation died in the wilderness because of their unbelief. The journey of the nation of Israel in the wilderness exposes the oppressive, slavery spirit and mindset the nation of Israel carried inwardly. Though they were outwardly free from the oppression and slavery of the Egyptians, in the wilderness God wanted them to get rid of the mindset they had while they were in Egypt and introduce them to His ways of thinking based on His covenant, character, and promise He made to their forefathers, Abraham, Isaac and Jacob (see Deuteronomy 7:7-8) (see Isaiah 55:8-11). For the nation of Israel, the battle to possess the promised land was no longer a fight against Pharaoh and the Egyptian army, but rather mindsets and belief systems they cultivated as slaves and opposed the promises of God. For 40 years, they did not have any physical enemy as their main threat; their biggest enemy was their mindset and unbelief. It was all about the battle of the mind; they were free but could not possess the land. The wilderness is a place where the Lord prepared His people for possessing the land. It is a place to rely and trust in the Lord. The number 40 in the bible is the number of trials. Israel spent 40 years in the wilderness. They were tested by the Lord to see if they would walk by faith and not by sight. Jesus fasted forty days and forty nights being tested and also tempted by the Devil (Matthew 4:2). Therefore, in the wilderness God prepares people to be spiritually, mentally and physically ready for the assignments He has assigned unto them. Even though the Lord used the wilderness as a place of preparation it was not part of the promise He made unto them (Exodus 3:8). Many Christians nowadays are too content with wilderness testimonies and have become too complacent, living on survival mode rather than abundance which is to go beyond the wilderness into their prophetic destiny. Israel lived below the promises of God because of unbelief, ignorance and stubbornness. While they were in Egypt, it seemed like the big problem was Pharaoh; yes Pharaoh oppressed them harshly, but when they were freed by the Lord supernaturally the moment they crossed the Red Sea their biggest enemy showed up and it was their mindset that hindered Israel from entering the promised land quickly. It was not Pharaoh or the devil, rather it was themselves. Prophetically the church is going through this same dilemma where the promises of God are Yes and Amen but it seems like the church has become stagnant like Israel in the wilderness for more than 40 years. It is time to begin to walk in the prophetic plans and timing of God; no more delays and procrastination. The Old Testament is a shadow of what is to come therefore the Old Testament contains prophetic insight about the church and her assignment. Jesus unveils in the gospel of Matthew 24:14 that the final sign of the end times is when the gospel of the kingdom is preached to all nations. This word "nation" in the Greek means more than just ethnicity, people groups. It also refers to different subdivisions of society such as government, economy, family, religion, media, education, arts and entertainment. According to Jesus we are to preach a message which is to reshape the society, not a message that will make people more religious. In fact Jesus never came to preach a religion rather He came to preach about the kingdom of God. The gospel of the kingdom is the message that Jesus preached everywhere He went (Matthew 4:17-23). The by-products were salvation, healing, deliverance, prosperity, governmental prosperity and healing of the land. When the church begins to fully understand, and preach this message we will see a revolution in the nations. The gospel of the kingdom is about God's kingdom being restored on earth as it is in heaven. The church carries the same commission Jesus carried while He was on earth; the promised land is nations being restored to the kingdom.

Six prophetic typologies of the church entering the promised land

The Apostle Paul in his writings to the Corinthians made it very clear that all the things that happened to Israel in the Old Testament are examples and warnings to us. If we do not learn from them we will repeat the same mistakes they made in the wilderness (1 Cor. 10:1-13). Typology and shadows are simply hidden mysteries that contain a concealed message about Jesus and the church in the Old Testament, therefore when we read and study the Old Testament we should be aware that God's blue print for salvation and restoring His kingdom on earth are hidden in characters and stories of the Old Testament. The story of Abraham sacrificing His son Isaac hides a mystery of God giving His only begotten son Jesus to come and be the sacrificial lamb who takes away the sin of the world (John 1:29). So then Isaac becomes a typology of Jesus in the Old Testament. He was also a miracle child (Genesis 22). The old testament books are full of many golden nuggets of truth that can only be revealed by the Holy

Salvation the seal of dominion

Spirit. Below we see six types and shadows about the journey of the nation of Israel from Egypt to the promised land and its significant relationship to the church.

- Israel typifies the believer, as the chosen people of God through a covenant Deuteronomy 7:7-8
- Egypt typifies the world system, and spiritual bondage Ephesians 2:2
- Pharaoh typifies Satan the ruler of this world system Ephesians 2:2
- Red Sea typifies redemption through the blood of Jesus and baptism typifies new life
- The wilderness typifies a place of being filtered, reshaped, trials, maturity and preparation
- The promised land typifies prophetic destiny

The promised Land

God gave the promised land in advance to Israel but they did not mix the word of the Lord with faith, therefore many failed to enter it and the few that entered also failed to possess the entire land due to unbelief and disobediences (see Joshua 1:1-4). The Lord told Joshua that every place the sole of his foot touched He would give him as inheritance. We see this prophetic declaration in the battle of Jericho. The Lord instructed Joshua and the entire nation to march around Jericho for six days, once a day, and on the seventh day they should march seven times (see Joshua 6). The possessing of the promised land is through faith in the word of God. The Lord revealed to Israel that they would face seven nations mightier than them, to possess the land given to them by the Lord (see Deuteronomy 7:1-8). These seven nations were Hittites, Girgashites, Amorites, Canaanites, Perizzites, Hivites and the Jebusites. The Lord promised to deliver these nations into the hands of Israel to fulfil His covenant promised to Abraham (see Genesis 15:13-14). The promise land was given to Israel through a covenant and they failed to understand this privilege of being the beneficiaries of the promised inheritance. At many times, we can relate to the nation of Israel with the challenges they faced, the promised land is the prophetic destiny the Lord has promised to all His sons and daughters in the kingdom. The Lord wants us to walk in our prophetic destiny and purpose. Many believers become content with the wilderness blessings such as manna, quails and lifestyle because of the survival spirit; the manna from heaven with all the miracle provisions were just a taste of what was to come. The Lord gave specific promises about the promised land. He said, "It will be a land which flows with milk and honey". It is not a land of lack and survival; it requires a new way of thinking not a backward mindset. To possess your promised land, you need a new revelation from the Lord. You cannot walk into your destiny with a revelation from your past experiences. For some it may mean to let go of their own ambitions and plans and start asking the Lord "What is your blue print for me to possess my promise land?" (Isaiah 43:19). When you begin to seek the Lord to order your steps, He will make your path clear even in the darkest and most confusing moments of your life. The nation of Israel was led by a pillar of cloud by day and a pillar of fire by night signifying the infinite knowledge of God about His directions, plans and purpose towards His people. The book of Proverbs makes it clear that there is a way that seems right to humans but at the end it leads to death. When the Lord leads He goes ahead of you, and clears the way from all things that want to choke you entering your prophetic destiny, the promised land. Entering your promised land requires childlike attitudes. You have to let go of all you know and start a journey of trust and faith. Total dependency on the Lord means a constant reminder to self that it's going to be alright when it seems to be impossible, and beyond. Faith is standing on the word and declaring to your problems, circumstances, mountains and challenges that it does not matter how it may look or feel like, but because God said it shall come to pass, it will come to pass for He is not a man that He should lie or a son of man to change His mind (Numbers 23:19). The battle over the promised land is a battle of faith. The enemy uses natural circumstances to intimidate you and look at your size, past, family and inabilities for he knows the more you dwell and meditate on the promises of God, you will have no room for fear. When Moses sent out the twelve spies, ten came back with bad reports' saying that they cannot defeat their enemies that were living in the promised land because they were big and the Israelites looked like grass hoppers in their eyes. These are words of fear and the enemy wants the people of God to confess their weakness and circumstances instead of declaring the promises of the Lord to the enemy. Only two people came back without fear. Joshua and Caleb, despite all the negative things they saw, believed what the Lord said. Faith does not deny circumstances; faith is not wishful thinking to deny what you see, rather it's acknowledging that, yes your circumstances in the natural look bad but because of God they will turn around for your good. Joshua and Caleb had faith in God. They could have chosen to break down and give in to fear. Faith makes you rule over circumstances. Jesus, when He was tempted by the Devil in the wilderness in His fast for forty days and forty nights, did not tell the Devil His circumstances such as hunger, thirst, or lack of proper sleep, but He spoke the word of God and He overcame the enemy through speaking the word of God (see Matthew 4:1-11). The ten out of the twelve spies were intimidated by the descendants of Anak (Numbers 13:33). The name **"Anak"** means **'choke'** or **'strangle',** as if something is choking you on your neck like a necklace. Fear is a weapon that the enemy uses mostly to strangle our faith to enter the promised land. The descendants of Anak choked the faith out of the ten men; only two men refused to be choked by fear. The word 'fear' can be broken with each of the letters spelling a word. False. Evidence. Appearing. Real. The enemy always comes to paint a picture of your imperfections and past to take your focus from God's faithfulness. The moment we become so consumed with ourselves, that makes a room for him to enter. There are three strategies the enemy uses. We can learn from the descendants of **Anak** who typify the enemy; the three sons of **Anak** were **Ahiman**, **Sheshai** and **Talmai.** These names carry prophetic insight about the tactics the enemy uses to cripple the believer's faith to enter their promised land. The first name **Ahiman,** means 'block' or 'hindrance', signifying that the enemy wants to block and delay God's plans and purpose for His people to enter in to the promised land. The second name **Sheshai** means 'white wash' (see Matthew 23:27), disguise or camouflage, signifying that the enemy always uses fear which is false evidence appearing real to convince God's people to accept living outside God's perfect will, the promised land, and settle for less. The last name **Talmai,** means 'accumulate' signifying that the enemy wants God's people to be so busy with what looks right so they will waste their time. These are three strategies Israel had to overcome when they were challenged by the descendants of Anak. The battle over the promised land or your prophetic destiny requires you to have the right perspective which is the ability to visualise and imagine the promised land being given to you already by the Lord. When Abraham was in doubt about the promises of God, the Lord told him to look up and count the stars in the heavens. Here we can learn that God is a visual God. He wants His people to always see things in the spirit before they manifest in the natural (see Genesis 15:5 to see as He sees). Your mind needs to conceive a new imagination of the reality of the promise God made. Israel crossed the Red Sea but still carried the vision of Pharaoh, of slavery beyond the Red Sea in their hearts and minds. The lesson is, Don't allow your mind to be occupied with anything that is not of God's plan. Pharaoh was still controlling the mindsets of Israel even though they were free from the bondage of slavery. It takes constant transformation and renewal of the mind to completely visualise and believe the word of the Lord as the reality.

Conquering the seven mighty nations

Israel had to face seven mighty nations that dwelled in Canaan land, to possess their given inheritance, the promised land. The Lord promised to drive out the seven nations little by little, until Israel completely took over the land (see Deuteronomy 7). The seven nations were the **Hittites, Girgashites, Amorites, Canaanites, Perizzites, Hivites and Jebusites**. These seven nations prophetically represent the seven systematic enemies. Sons and daughters of God in the kingdom must conquer to possess their inheritance, the promised land. The name **Hittites** means fear or terror. This nation prophetically speaks of how the enemy uses fear to stop many from entering their promised land which God has given them. In His plans and purposes, He called many, to be great entrepreneurs, lawyers, sport super stars, apostles and prophets and so forth, but because of fear, many get choked from believing to strive to the destiny they are called to. Today in our society the biggest platform the enemy is using is the spirit of the Hittites. The media projects fear and false news to alarm and create a fearful society. Every day on the news journalists and news reporters only report and focus on bad news such as wars, the economy collapsing, the increase of the job crisis, increase of suicide so that the people's mind will be full of fear and terror. The spirit of fear kills dreams, vision and determination within the heart of men and women. The enemy knows that if he fills your mind and heart with fear and doubt he has you under his control. The way to conquer the Hittites' spirit is to constantly wear the helmet of salvation, renewing our minds with the truth of God's word about His goodness, grace and faithfulness. One of the characteristics of the enemy is deception. He twists things, therefore many believe his lies because they make sense. These are what I call logical lies, or strongholds. For example the enemy may tell you that you should not give ten percent of your income to the Lord because life is hard and things are tight. This may sound logical enough as a valid point, but what he fails to mention is that God is the owner of all the earth including you (see Psalms 24). Therefore God tests us with the greatest idol and value humanity lives for-money-, to see which is more important, money or Him (see Matthew 6:19-24). When you get this right you will never lack financially because you are worshipping Him with your finances, and the love of money does not take your heart away from Him. On the other hand, the logical lie the enemy tells believers is that God did not work for this money so why should I give him ten percent of my hard-earned income? When you believe this lie you miss out on the blessings He has promised specifically about finances (see Proverbs 3:9-10 Luke 5:38 2 Cor. 9:6-8). We must be alert about opening doors to the enemy through lies and fear. The spirit of the Hittites is a spirit that releases terror and fear against your promised land.

Salvation the seal of dominion 93

The name **Girgashites** means **dwellers of the clay**. This represents being led by the flesh and earthly ambitions. The spirit behind the **Girgashites** prophetically speaks of how the enemy uses a religious spirit to oppress the people of God from entering the promised land. Religious people are always busy with rituals and traditions. They do not give the Holy Spirit room to guide and lead them to their prophetic destiny. The nation of Israel was walking in the flesh, therefore it took them longer to possess the promised land. Walking in the flesh, which represents your human strength and ability, will burn you out. It takes the grace and power of God to walk into what God has called you (see Zachariah 4:6).

The name **Amorites** means **pride** and **rebellion**. The spirit behind this nation prophetically speaks of rebellion and unbelief against God's promises and purpose. This spirit also exalts humanistic ideologies over God's word. It is secular focussed, and the ways of God require faith and revelation not humanistic philosophy. The Amorites lived in caves on high mountains representing self-exaltation. True promotion comes from the Lord not from humans. When human beings lift you up they will immediately bring you down before the day ends (see Psalms 75:6-7). We can only defeat and conquer the spirit of the Amorites through trust and humility, not religious humility of self-pity, but humility of total dependency on the Lord's strength to guide you to His promise, your destiny (see Proverbs 3:5).

The name **Canaanites** means **materialism.** The spirit behind this nation prophetically speaks of putting the things of this world before God. The first and foremost goal of every believer is to seek first the kingdom of God and His righteousness, and the rest shall come afterwards, In the wilderness, the children of Israel were worshipping idols things that they made with their hands such as the golden calf. Today in the body of Christ there are many golden calves that have been put in place of God as idols. God is restoring the apostolic and prophetic ministries to bring a divine alignment to the body of Christ. In 2 kings chapter six we see the sons of the prophets cutting wood to build a house. But as they were busy working, one of the axe-heads fell into the water and it took a miracle from the Prophet Elisha to make the axe-head float and be found. This story carries a prophetic insight about God restoring the apostolic and prophetic as the cutting edge leading ministries back to the body of Christ. For many years past religion has taught people to believe that apostles and prophets ceased, but this is not scripturally accurate. Apostolic and Prophetic ministries are needed in every generation to bring alignment, order, spiritual covering, leadership and supernatural impartation (see 1 Cor. 12:27-28 Ephesians 2:21-20). In our 21st century, many ministers who lack apostolic and prophetic leadership lose focus on the original mission of God, which is a kingdom mandate. Some have made a materialistic focused gospel replace the kingdom message of heaven invading the earth. Having great things is not bad, but what is dangerous is when the materialistic things of this world become the goal and the focus of the Christian life. God has already promised us that if we seek Him and His kingdom first all things shall be added unto us (see Matthew 6:33). The materialistic spirit makes people become focused on having more, to become more, and this is a very dangerous mindset to have. Your worth as a child of God is not based on what you have and what you do not have. Rather it is based on your creator God. To overcome and conquer the spirit of the Canaanites, we must have a balanced understanding of biblical prosperity, which is to be rich and wealthy spiritually, mentally, emotionally, financially, relationally and physically. The

Salvation the seal of dominion

promised land comes with abundance of blessings. The people of this world have all the materialistic things such as nice houses, cars, and so forth but they are still poor. The true fulfilment of promised land is to accomplish the purpose of God which is your prophetic destiny; materials are part of the resource package the Lord gives you to live a fulfilled life.

The name **Perizzites**, means opened or unprotected. The spirit behind this nation prophetically speaks of liberalism, religion and false doctrines. The church of Jesus needs to be more discerning than ever before because of the great deception that is taking place in the church. Many religious and humanistic beliefs are being accepted by the church of Jesus Christ in the name of being relevant. The spirit of the Perizzites can only be destroyed through strong prophetic and apostolic prayer of releasing heaven on earth as the church begins to pray kingdom prayers not religious prayers. The strongholds of liberalism, religion and false doctrine will be destroyed through the anointing of the Holy Spirit (see Matthew 6:10). The Perizzites want to destroy the wall of your values, principles, family, trust in God so that you become vulnerable and a victim of the enemy. God has given you the Holy Spirit to guide, lead and counsel you constantly in every phase of your life, therefore fear not any attacks of the enemy. "You shall see danger from afar but it shall not come near you will only be a spectator". This is a promise the Lord has made as a weapon to defeat the enemy (see Psalm 91).

The name **Hivites** means **lies, deception or falsehood** (see Genesis 34:1-2). The spirit behind this nation prophetically speaks of deception. The enemy is always counterfeiting what is of God to trick and mislead the people of God. Being aligned with God prophetically is the key to conquering the spirit of the Hivites. David in his time of critical decision always consulted

God for prophetic directions. The enemy hates when you ask the Lord for divine directions for he knows the Lord knows the end from the beginning and his plans get exposed (see 2 Samuel 5:17-19 John 16:13). The **Gibeonites**, who were **Hivites**, deceived Joshua to make a covenant to not harm or kill them. Joshua did not consult the Lord before making a covenant with them, therefore he was deceived and he made a covenant with his enemies because of the lack of discernment (see Joshua 9). Before you make decisions concerning anything, including major decisions, seek the Lord for direction. The spirit of Hivites is out there to deceive and delay the people of God from entering the promised land.

The name **Jebusites** means **trodden down or rejection.** The spirit behind this nation prophetically speaks of great discouragement. The enemy is out there to attack the people of God through guilt, condemnation, rejection and the past so that they do not make it to their prophetic destiny. The Lord has promised that He will never leave or forsake you child of God, even during the fire of life or family trials. The Jebusite spirit is out there to make you feel like God is no longer with you in your journey. The journey of the Israelites from Egypt is a good illustration of the faithfulness of God towards His people. He led them by a pillar of cloud by day and a pillar of fire by night. God's presence will always be with you even when you are discouraged. The enemy is after discouraging you from entering your promised land but you are an overcomer in Christ Jesus, and the enemy is under your feet (see Hebrews 13:4).

Prophetic keys to walk to your promise Land

- Understand your purpose and assignment from God
- Walk by faith 2 Corinthians 5:7

- Warfare in the spirit through spiritual force of prayer and faith
- The armour of salvation Ephesians 6
- Prophetic insight about times and seasons 1 Chronicles 12:32
- Supernatural focus and determination
- Divine connections

The bigger picture, the kingdom, and the church

The vision of God is bigger than just attending church. Nowadays churches have become so content with emphasis on growing in numbers which is not a bad thing, but it can become dangerous when it replaces the original vision of Jesus and become the focus. There are small churches that justify their small numbers because they claim to focus on spiritual growth and that they are not concerned about quantity but rather, quality. On the other hand, there are mega churches – full of people but in depth very shallow. The goal of God is to both grow and be strong spiritually and numerically, as well to remain focus on the kingdom agenda not church(see Acts 9:31). The word church comes from the Greek word Ecclesia and this word literally means the gathering of elite groups which were politicians, public figures, the rich and the upper class. The church is not a building that people meet on Sunday. It is the gathering of the most powerful people on earth who are called to bring change by God, with this definition I am not implying that you have to be a celebrity, millionaire, public figure to be used by God but it means that God sees all his children powerful and cable of attaining all the promises he has made about changing the world. In the gospel of Mark 11 Jesus whipped and cast people out who turned the house of God into a market place where they used it for business rather than empowering the kingdom community, to have dynamic ministries to minister the love of God to a dying world. Today in the church these same spirits are at a work perverting believers, ministers and leaders to become more oriented with church administrations such as things like buildings. Large auditoriums have now become the vision of some pastors because some want to have a mega church, while all these things in the eyes of God mean nothing. God is looking for and raising people who are kingdom oriented not church focused. In this season, God is bringing divine alignment to His prophetic purposes; there is apostolic and prophetic revolution taking place. Truths are being restored back to the body of Christ that have been ignored for many decades and generations because of the religious spirits that have entered the church. The church must change her ways of thinking and embrace what God is doing in the now. One of the biggest challenges that has hindered the church from seeing the bigger picture, is the fear of change and religious mindsets. Therefore, many are hiding behind the walls of their denominations as though that was the mission of God. The church is the light of the world and a light cannot be hidden, rather it has to be placed where it can be seen by all who are lost in darkness. Child of God, you are called at such time as this to be part of a global change. You are called with high calling to represent the King of kings and the Lords of lords Jesus Christ. Go and change the nations through the message of Christ; that is The Great Commission.

Reflective thoughts and questions about being part of the bigger picture

- **Am I born again?**
  Salvation in the bible is the central theme of God for humanity, it's God seeking to restore relationship with his creation. He wants us to be in eternal fellowship with Him. To be born

Salvation the seal of dominion

again is not to enter your mother's womb second time and be reborn, but it's to be born within through the regenerating of your inner person who is dead in sin by receiving God's love (Jesus Christ) who paid the price of redemption through His blood. The bible reveals that the wages of sin is death and the gift of God is eternal life through Jesus Christ (Romans 6:23).

If you have said No to this first question, just simply pray this heart felt prayer of salvation and today you will experience the love and of the father and receive sonship (John 3:16).

Dear heavenly Father,

Thank you for demonstrating your love by manifesting yourself in your son Jesus. Thank you for dying on the cross for my sin. Thank you for forgiving my sin. Come into my life Lord Jesus. I receive you as my Lord and Saviour. I invite your Spirit to come and help me live for you for the rest of my life.

In the name of Jesus, I pray.
Amen

- How can I be part of this bigger picture?
- Where am I called the market place, five-fold ministry, sports and so forth?
- Without God man cannot, and without man God will not.

End notes

Munroe, Myles. Rediscovering the Kingdom Expanded Edition. Destiny Image. Kindle Edition.

Munroe, Myles. Understanding Your Place in God's Kingdom: Your Original Purpose for Destiny Image. Kindle Edition.

Kenyon, E.W. Two Kinds of Righteouness. Lynnwood, Wash. Kenyons Gospel Publishing, 1996.

Hankins, Mark. *Paul's System of Truth*. Edited by Mark Hankins Ministries staff. 1st edition. Mark Hankins Publishers, 2010.

Hagin, K. E. Growing Up Spiritually. Faith Library Publications, Incorporated, 1982. https://books.google.com.au/books?id=xVkFAAAACAAJ.

Enlow, J. *The Seven Mountain Prophecy: Unveiling the Coming Elijah Revolution*. Charisma House, 2015. https://books.google.com.au/books?id=yZ3MCgAAQBAJ.

www.ingramcontent.com/pod-product-compliance
Lightning Source LLC
Chambersburg PA
CBHW051954290426
44110CB00015B/2244